Desperate Faith

Desperate Faith

by
Howard M. Harper, Jr.

— a study of BELLOW

SALINGER

MAILER

BALDWIN

and

UPDIKE

THE UNIVERSITY OF
NORTH CAROLINA PRESS • CHAPEL HILL

Thanks are due to the following publishers for permission to quote from the authors and works indicated:

Beacon Press for James Baldwin's *Notes of a Native Son*
The Dial Press, Inc., for Norman Mailer's *An American Dream*
Holt, Rinehart and Winston, Inc., for Norman Mailer's *Barbary Shore* and *The Naked and the Dead*
Alfred A. Knopf, Inc., for John Updike's *Assorted Prose, The Centaur, Of the Farm, The Poorhouse Fair,* and *Rabbit, Run*
G. P. Putnam's Sons for Norman Mailer's *Advertisements of Myself, The Deer Park,* and *The Presidential Papers*
Vanguard Press, Inc., for Saul Bellow's *Dangling Man* and *The Victim*
Other works by Saul Bellow: *The Adventures of Augie March,* copyright © 1949, 1951, 1952, 1953 by Saul Bellow; *Henderson the Rain King,* copyright © 1958, 1959 by Saul Bellow; *Herzog,* copyright © 1961, 1963, 1964 by Saul Bellow; *Seize the Day,* copyright © 1951, 1954, 1955, 1956 by Saul Bellow; all reprinted by permission of The Viking Press, Inc.
Other works by James Baldwin: Reprinted from *Go Tell It on the Mountain* by James Baldwin. Copyright © 1952, 1953 by James Baldwin and used with permission of the publisher, The Dial Press, Inc. Reprinted from *Another Country* by James Baldwin. Copyright © 1960, 1962 by James Baldwin and used with permission of the publisher, The Dial Press, Inc. Reprinted from *Nobody Knows My Name* by James Baldwin. Copyright © 1954, 1956, 1958, 1960, 1961 and used with permission of the publisher, The Dial Press, Inc. Reprinted from *Giovanni's Room* by James Baldwin. Copyright © 1956 by James Baldwin and used with permission of the publisher, The Dial Press, Inc. Reprinted from *The Fire Next Time* by James Baldwin. Copyright © 1962, 1963 by James Baldwin and used with the permission of the publisher, The Dial Press, Inc.

Acknowledgements

Special thanks for help in the preparation of this book are due to: Professor Arthur O. Lewis, Jr., of The Pennsylvania State University for his advice in the planning of this study and for his insight, criticism, and encouragement; Professor Louis D. Rubin, Jr., of Hollins College for his perceptive reading of the manuscript; my colleague James E. Bryan II of The University of North Carolina at Chapel Hill for his generosity in sharing his impressive knowledge of Salinger and for his criticism of Chapter 3; and The University of North Carolina Press for its comprehensive and painstaking assistance.

Contents

Desperate Faith

one

Introduction

The only requirement for good fiction, Henry James said, is that it be interesting. Although the writer of fiction must work with a publisher and within the law, he has no legal obligation to be doctrinaire, logical, or even coherent. Because his story is assumed to be an imaginary one, he can tell it without regard for the formal rules of evidence. In a society in which truth is "managed," this is not a minor freedom.

Classic fiction is good fiction which remains interesting. It is relevant not only to its own time, but to all time. Although such novels as *The Scarlet Letter, Moby-Dick, Huckleberry Finn, Sister Carrie, The Sun Also Rises,* and *The Sound and the Fury* were revolutionary technical achievements, they are classics today because they deal with universal questions in unique and interesting ways. They express what Paul Tillich called ultimate concern.

Our best contemporary fiction also has this quality of ultimate concern. With this concern, with their impressive talents, and with their almost unlimited freedom, our best contemporary writers are recording, as artists always have, their responses to the ultimate ques-tions. These questions need not be an explicit purpose of art, but they are an inevitable product of it. In the English lan-guage, the most profound commentary on the human condi-tion was written not by a philosopher but by a playwright —and presumably to make money. It is precisely because art is not required to make a case for anything that it achieves its unique truth; since it is not committed to making systematic sense, it is able to show, as no other medium of expression can, not only how things should be, but how they really are.

But even though every work of art is unique, we can still associate certain general ideas with certain periods in literary history. Every era has its own climate of ideas; in this climate the artist must live and, through his own unique personal vision, transform his experience into the work of art. Although he may oppose popular, institutionalized values, he must still respond to them and to the universal problems which he, simply as a human being, shares with the men of his time. The artist's responses to these problems, the problems in-volved in what Malraux has called *la condition humaine,* give his work its most enduring interest. And certain patterns of responses have been dominant in certain eras. It is these patterns which enable us to talk meaningfully about broad literary and philosophical movements, such as Transcenden-talism or Existentialism, which involve many unique personal-ities who nevertheless respond similarly to the ultimate questions.

This book is a study of the responses of five of our best contemporary writers to these questions. Because the ultimate stature of our contemporaries can only be guessed at, a broad survey of contemporary fiction seems less desirable than a closer look at a few writers. These five were chosen from a group of fifteen or twenty who have emerged since World War II and whose importance has been rather widely recognized.

Saul Bellow, winner of two National Book Awards, now has the largest reputation among these novelists. He is one of the older members of the group; his first novel was published in

1944, and he had made his commitment to literature in 1937. From the beginning his work has shown ultimate concern, and it has grown dramatically in style and richness throughout his career.

Although the reputation of J. D. Salinger is now declining, the "Salinger industry" is still booming. While it is currently fashionable to call him a minor writer, the great amount of critical attention and the wide audience which his work has received seem to indicate that it has touched some of the most sensitive nerves of the contemporary consciousness.

Norman Mailer is ignored by some critics, patronized by some, and given very close and respectful attention by others. While his popular stock has declined since the tremendous success of *The Naked and the Dead,* his later journey of exploration into the darkest recesses of the self has shown not only courage and integrity, but also an acute sense of judgment. His style is exciting, and his insights are often deep and startling.

The Negro writer necessarily sees the human condition from a much different point of view than the white writer. Although there are many white Americas, the frontiers between them are not as strongly guarded as the wall which separates them from the black Americas. On the far side of this racial wall, beyond the view of white writers, lies an increasingly significant part of American experience. James Baldwin is now the leading literary spokesman for the Negro. Although Ralph Ellison's *Invisible Man* is far better than anything Baldwin has written, it is Ellison's only novel thus far. Baldwin, with three novels and a number of influential essays—not to mention his stories and plays—has been more prolific and a more militant crusader for civil rights. It is for these reasons that he was selected for this study.

Finally, it seemed desirable to include a younger writer, a novelist whose reputation is only now becoming established. John Updike, born in 1932, was the obvious choice. His four novels, one of which won a National Book Award, and three volumes of short stories have marked the beginnings of a major reputation. Updike has always had impressive style and sensibility, and his work in the 1960's shows a deepening concern with the ultimate questions.

Obviously this selection of writers is subjective and somewhat arbitrary. It excludes Ellison, Flannery O'Connor, Bernard Malamud, Eudora Welty, Wright Morris, Paul Bowles, and probably others whom later generations will consider in qualitative discussions of American fiction of the two decades since World War II. Nevertheless, the writers selected are among the best of this period, and they are engaged in highly interesting ways with the most vital issues of our time. Taken as a whole their work provides, if not a comprehensive index, at least a powerful and valuable insight into the human condition in America today.

two

SAUL BELLOW
– the heart's ultimate need

In 1941 Saul Bellow published his first story in the *Partisan Review*. "Two Morning Monologues" [1] is interesting because it defines the polar situation in which all of Bellow's later heroes are caught. The first monologue is that of a young man who, like the hero of Bellow's first novel, is waiting for his draft call, and indeed would welcome it as an end to his drifting. The second is the monologue of a horseplayer who is also obsessed with his lack of identity: "Who picks us out?" he wonders. "Who decides or what decides my place . . . ?" His compulsive betting is an attempt to assert his freedom: "Manage right and never die. . . . It's in your hands and in your power."

These two themes—of man adrift in a world he never made, and of man's yearning for transcendent power —are the horns of the now familiar existential dilemma.

1. Saul Bellow, "Two Morning Monologues," *Partisan Review*, VIII (May–June, 1941), 230–36.

And the behavior of Bellow's two monologuists—aimless drifting by the one and compulsive, gratuitous action by the other
—is characteristic of Bellow's later heroes, as well as of existential heroes in general.[2] Although these themes are almost
cliches today, Bellow's story was written in an America
which had not yet read Camus and whose literature still
echoed the calls to social and political action. In 1941 existentialism was not yet a cultural movement even in France, although its major themes had been sounded in the work of
Malraux, and had caught the attention of intellectuals in the
United States.[3]

Bellow's first novel, *Dangling Man* (1944), explores the
dilemma which the earlier story had suggested. The protagonist's lack of identity is emphasized. His first name is Joseph,
but we never learn his last name, though a number of critics
have suggested that he is related to Kafka's Joseph K. The
novel is the journal which he keeps from December 15, 1942,
to April 9, 1943, his last day in civilian life. At the time of the
first entry he has been "dangling" between the civilian and
military worlds for about seven months. Because he is a
Canadian alien, he cannot be drafted without an investigation, and the red tape has delayed his induction to the point

2. For discussions of the existential hero in contemporary American
fiction, see Richard Lehan, "Existentialism in Recent American Fiction:
The Demonic Quest," *Texas Studies in Literature and Language*, I
(Summer 1959), 181–202; Ihab Hassan, *Radical Innocence: Studies in
the Contemporary American Novel* (Princeton: Princeton University
Press, 1961), and his "The Existential Novel," *Massachusetts Review*,
III (Summer, 1962), 795–97; and David Galloway, *The Absurd Hero in
American Fiction* (Austin: University of Texas Press, 1966), a study of
Updike, Styron, Bellow, and Salinger.

3. As a student at Harvard, Norman Mailer wrote a short novel
influenced by *Man's Fate*. In France "it was Malraux, through his novels,
who shaped the sensibilities which then seized on doctrinal Existentialism
as an ideological prop," according to Joseph Frank, "Andre Malraux: The
Image of Man," *Hudson Review*, XIV (Spring 1961), 50. For an
excellent discussion of existentialism by a philosopher with impressive
literary insights, see William Barrett, *Irrational Man: A Study in
Existential Philosophy* (New York: Doubleday, 1958). For a bibliography
of the literary aspects of the existential movement, see Richard Lehan,
"French and American Philosophical and Literary Existentialism: A
Selected Check List," *Wisconsin Studies in Contemporary Literature*, I,
iii (Fall 1960), 74–88.

that it seems the war has passed him by. On the assumption that he would soon be called into service, he had quit his job and is living on the income of his wife Iva, a librarian.

The dangling man must use his own resources to fill the void which his withdrawal from society has created. But his isolation and unhappiness only become more pronounced, and the novel ends with his volunteering for the army. He had been reluctant to do so because enlistment would be an admission of his inability to use his freedom, and a tacit acceptance of responsibility for involvement in the war. He would rather have been drafted and absolved of responsibility. His attitude toward the war is summarized in his entry for January 4:

I would rather die in the war than consume its benefits. When I am called I shall go and make no protest. And, of course, I hope to survive. But I would rather be a victim than a beneficiary. I support the war, though it is perhaps gratuitous to say so; we have the habit of making these things issues of personal morality and private will, which they are not at all. The equivalent would be to say, if God really existed, yes, God does exist. He would exist whether we recognized him or not. But as between their imperialism and ours, if a full choice were possible, I would take ours. Alternatives, and particularly desirable alternatives, grow only on imaginary trees.

Yes, I shall shoot, I shall take lives; I shall be shot at, and my life may be taken. Certain blood will be given for half-certain reasons, as in all wars. Somehow I cannot regard it as a wrong against myself.

Since the international crisis is not a matter of "private will," the question confronting Joseph is whether a separate identity is possible in a world in which war dominates the national life. He sees his friends drawn into the conflict one by one, either directly, like Jefferson Forman who is killed in the South Pacific and Morris Abt who is turning out pamphlets in Washington, or indirectly, like his brother Amos and the tailor Fanzell who are profiting by it. Joseph compares the war to the ravages of bacteria: "I am concerned with them, naturally. I must take account of them. They can obliterate me. But as long as I am alive, I must follow my destiny in spite of them." He makes his statement in a talk with the Spirit of Alternatives, an inner voice with which he confers in moments of stress. The Spirit then poses the crucial question: "Whether you have a separate destiny. . . ." Joseph confesses that "I'm not ready to answer. I have nothing to say to that now."

Joseph is a philosopher by avocation; he had been writing a series of essays on the philosophers of the Enlightenment, but his essay on Diderot was interrupted by his first call from the draft board and never resumed. As a close student of the Enlightenment, he wishes to believe in the power of reason as a philosophy of life. But he is fully aware of the consequences of an unlimited faith in reason. Since—if the doctrine of the Enlightenment is carried to its logical conclusion—it is man rather than God who ultimately determines his fate, man is placed under an overwhelming responsibility. In this responsibility, too grave for man to face as an insistent daily fact of life, Joseph recognizes the roots of the pervasive modern terror and insecurity:

It is because we have been taught there is no limit to what a man can be. Six hundred years ago, a man was what he was born to be. Satan and the Church, representing God, did battle over him. He, by reason of his choice, partially decided the outcome. But whether, after life, he went to hell or to heaven, his place among other men was given. . . . But, since, the stage has been reset and human beings only walk on it, and, under this revision, we have, instead, history to answer to. . . . Now, each of us is responsible for his own salvation, which is in his greatness. And that, that greatness, is the rock our hearts are abraded on. . . . we hate immoderately and punish ourselves and one another immoderately. The fear of lagging pursues and maddens us. The fear lies in us like a cloud. It makes an inner climate of darkness.

It is this overwhelming responsibility which Joseph, despite his keen mind, his courage, and his will, cannot live with. Although he is able to carry on his struggle for almost a year, he finally chooses the comfortable irresponsibility which the army affords.

It is important to recognize the real reason for this choice: Joseph's loss of his "place among men." Paradoxically, in giving up his stubborn fight for "identity," he achieves his true identity. His life can have real meaning only in relation to other lives. As his isolation grows more pronounced, he begins to speak of himself in the past tense and in the third person, as if "Joseph" were merely the name of his former identity. For example, at one point in the analysis of his former character, he says "To turn now to Joseph's dress (I am wearing his cast-off clothes), it adds to his appearance of maturity." The protagonist has become, like Dostoevski's underground man, nameless. His insistence upon his identity and individuality have made him a different man from the "Joseph" whom his wife, relatives, and friends knew; their relationships with him are based upon their understanding of an earlier "Joseph" who no longer exists, and these relationships deteriorate. The more he insists upon his identity,[4] the less successful he is in maintaining it.

Joseph had been in rebellion against his own humanity because what he has seen of humanity is not good enough. Beneath the ugly surface of life in wartime he is searching for some unifying values which he can live by, which will safeguard his identity against destruction by the dehumanizing forces he sees everywhere. His search is desperate; he realizes that "My beliefs are inadequate, they do not guard me . . . against the chaos I am forced to face." Without belief, life is reduced to a series of indistinguishable days, full of routine and empty of meaning. But even an inferior meaning, he finally decides, is better than none at all. This is the desperate need which pervades his journal, the need for an

ideal construction, an obsessive device. There have been innumerable varieties: for study, for wisdom, bravery, war, the benefits of cruelty, for art; the God-man of the ancient cultures, the

---

4. In a restaurant with Myron Adler, for example, Joseph becomes incensed because an old Communist acquaintance of his ignores him. "I have a right to be spoken to," he shouts. "It's the most elementary thing in the world." In much the same way, the refusal of a bank manager to honor Joseph's identification in cashing his wife's paycheck provokes him to an emotional outburst; he takes the manager's refusal as a personal affront and denial of his identity.

Humanistic full man, the courtly lover, the knight, the ecclesiastic, the despot, the ascetic, the millionaire, the manager. I could name hundreds of these ideal constructions, each with its assertions and symbols, each finding—in conduct, in God, in art, in money—its particular answer and each proclaiming: "This is the only possible way to meet chaos."

Finally, near the end of his journal, he concludes that "the highest 'ideal construction' is the one that unlocks the imprisoning self." By this time he has realized that he cannot conquer external chaos, but that he must adjust his own goals and values to those of the rest of humanity.

But in view of the apparent chaos and conflicting ideologies of modern society, can we assume that any basic goals and values really exist? Joseph has come to believe that we can: "The quest, I am beginning to think . . . is one and the same. I do not entirely understand this impulse. But it seems to me that its final end is the desire for pure freedom. We are all drawn toward the same craters of the spirit—to know what we are and what we are for, to know our purpose, to seek grace. And, if the quest is the same, the differences in our personal histories, which hitherto meant so much to us, become of minor importance."

Joseph's statement is partly wishful thinking. Even if the goals of the spirit are indeed the most important and the desire for "pure freedom" is the ultimate one, it does not follow that the differences in our personal histories become of little importance. Indeed, it is these very differences in values and attitudes which are isolating Joseph from his wife, his relatives, and his friends. These differences, in fact, have produced the chaos which Joseph is fleeing from.

Joseph himself in a sense acknowledges these differences when he notes that "goodness is achieved not in a vacuum, but in the company of other men, attended by love." This connection with mankind is what Joseph is seeking when he enlists in the army. In a talk with the Spirit of Alternatives he says that it is "important to know whether I can claim the right to preserve myself in this flood of death that has carried off so many like me. . . . It is appropriate to ask whether I have any business withholding myself from the same fate."

Although he eventually re-establishes the connection with mankind, he has realized from the beginning that it must be established within practical limits. In breaking off his love affair with Kitty Daumler, Joseph writes, "I made it clear that a man must accept limits and cannot give in to the wild desire to be everything and everyone and everything to everyone."

The ultimate limitation placed upon men, and the one which haunts Joseph's dreams, is death. In the journal entry for January 26, he recounts several dreams, in two of which a personification of death had appeared. This concern with death has its origin in an incident which had occurred six days before. Joseph had been walking to meet his wife for their anniversary dinner, and had seen a man stricken in the street. The event reminded him of his mother's death, and caused him to become preoccupied with man's mortality: "We know we are sought and expect to be found. . . . Who does not know him, the one who takes your measure in the street or on the stairs, he whose presence you must ignore in the darkened room if you are to close your eyes and fall asleep, the agent who takes you, in the last unforgiving act, into inexistence?"

When we become aware that we may, like the man Joseph saw in the street, be snatched at any moment into "inexistence," we see life itself with a new and compelling intensity. If the time between birth and death is all the time we have, then we must make the most of it. It is this fact, Joseph feels, which lies beneath our "bottomless avidity. Our lives are so precious to us, we are so watchful of waste. . . . Shall my life by one-thousandth of an inch fall short of its ultimate possibility? It is a different thing to value oneself, and to prize oneself crazily. And then there are our plans, idealizations. These are dangerous, too. They can consume us like parasites, eat us, drink us, and leave us lifelessly prostrate. And yet we are always inviting the parasite, as if we were eager to be drained and eaten." It is this avidity which Joseph sees as the central motive in human conflict. It motivates the struggle for money, power, and reputation in modern society. When

Amos, Joseph's status-conscious brother, tells him he should be practical and think of the future, Joseph replies that "There is no personal future any more." He means that the destinies of individuals have been swallowed up in mass conflicts which our own personal decisions cannot influence. Joseph's father argues that the liberal education which Joseph has acquired has prepared him for a life which is impossible to lead, and Joseph acknowledges that he is probably right: "I know now that I shall have to settle for very, very little. That is, I shall have to accept very little for there is no question of settling. Personal choice does not count for much these days."

Joseph's only real choices are those he makes in aligning himself with one faction or another in the vast conflicts which are reality. He cannot choose his fate; he can choose only how to interpret it. His instinctive interpretation, reinforced by his liberal education and his training in philosophy, is to reject the irrational. But he discovers that to reject the irrational is to reject much of life itself. Chaos, he finds, is a fact of life, and to insist upon rational order is to insist upon an existence which is other than human. Life must be lived not in terms of fixed, rational values, but in a constantly changing social context. His enlistment in the army is a surrender of his ideals and individuality, but also an acceptance of the basic facts of human existence. If it is cowardly in the first sense, it is courageous in the second, for it represents a rejection of a philosophical point of view which his life has shown to be untenable in favor of a new and untried set of values. The final entry in his journal is ironic in tone:

I am no longer to be held accountable for myself; I am grateful for that. I am in other hands, relieved of self-determination, freedom cancelled.
> Hurray for regular hours!
> And for the supervision of the spirit!
> Long live regimentation!

The increasing irony of this last entry moves away from the essential meaning of Joseph's enlistment. He has found instead that his stubborn insistence upon reason has carried him too far from humanity. His increasing isolation from his wife and friends, in the name of principle, has destroyed the very human values which he had hoped to enhance. He says that

there was an element of treason to common sense in the very objects of common sense. . . . there was no trusting them, save through wide agreement, and . . . my separation from such agreement had brought me perilously far from the necessary trust, auxiliary to all sanity. I had not done well alone. I doubted whether anyone could. To be pushed upon oneself entirely put the very facts of existence in doubt. . . . things were now out of my hands. The next move was the world's. I could not bring myself to regret it.

Dangling Man is a remarkable first novel. It represents a radical departure from the earlier traditions of American fiction; it is much closer to Dostoevski and Kafka than to Dos Passos, Hemingway, Farrell, Wolfe, Steinbeck, or other novelists whose reputations loomed so large at the time it was written. Because of its emphasis on the problems with which much of our later fiction would become obsessed, it seems almost prophetic.

The book is also an impressive technical achievement. Bellow's choice of the journal form is so right, so apparently natural, and now so widely used by other writers that we could easily overlook its originality in the American fiction of that period. The journal is the perfect form for the portrayal of a man imprisoned within his own mind, within an awareness of himself alone. Joseph's consciousness is the subject of the novel, and the journal form permits Bellow himself to maintain a certain distance from that consciousness at the same time that he makes the consciousness itself overwhelmingly immediate. Joseph's narcissism is not Bellow's own, and the fact that some reviewers complained of it shows how relatively new the narrative conception was.

The sharp focus on one character is typical of all of Bellow's later fiction. And Joseph is the prototype of the later heroes, suspended between uncertainties which he is afraid to accept and certainties in which he cannot believe. As in the later fiction, the need for acceptance proves to be the stronger because it involves the whole man—even the intellect, which, though far from satisfied, is now at least engaged with humanity rather than trapped in the stale prison of theorizing.

Bellow's second novel, *The Victim* (1947), in at least one way reverses the situation of *Dangling Man.* Joseph, obsessed with his philosophical needs, finds his personal experience falling apart. But Asa Leventhal, who had achieved a good five-cent synthesis, has it torn apart by personal experience. The most threatening of Leventhal's experiences are those involving Kirby Allbee, a former acquaintance who suddenly reappears with shrill accusations that Leventhal has ruined his life. Leventhal's experiences are the objective correlative through which Bellow explores the central problem of moral responsibility.

The Victim is told in the third person, but is focused upon Leventhal's perceptions; it does not enter into the minds of other characters or into scenes in which Leventhal is not present. This technique allows Bellow (rather than a narrator) to organize the events and to provide some atmospheric commentary; it achieves an immediacy approaching that of first-person narrative, but with tighter control. The first twenty-three chapters of the novel cover a period of about two weeks (with some additional background material) in Leventhal's life; the twenty-fourth chapter is an epilogue set on an evening several years later.

Leventhal, an editor for the Manhattan firm of Burke-Beard and Co., is a large, heavy, seemingly impassive man. But he is deeply sensitive and insecure. He views his modest success not as an accomplishment, but as something he "got away with." Because his formal education and manners are limited, and because he has known poverty and unemployment, he has a gripping fear of failure. "He felt that the harshness of his life had disfigured him, and that this disfigurement would be apparent." Sensitive also to the guarded anti-Semitism of his employers, he responds to it by withdrawing further.

Leventhal's brother Max is working in a Texas shipyard, and Max's wife Elena is worried about Mickey, their son, who has been ill for two weeks. Leventhal tries to persuade her to take the boy to a hospital, but cannot reason with her; he returns to his apartment filled with foreboding. His wife Mary is away with her recently widowed mother, and Leventhal is lonely and nervous. At this point in the story, through a series of fascinating coincidences,[5] Leventhal is confronted by Allbee and his wild accusations. Allbee had been fired after Leventhal had insulted Allbee's employer in an interview which Allbee had arranged for him; he had then gone from one disaster to another, until now, a derelict, he blames it all on Leventhal.

Conscious of being "singled out to be the object of some freakish, insane process," Leventhal heatedly rejects Allbee's charges, but is "filled with dread" because of his unconscious awareness that there may be some truth in them. Although he had never intended to hurt Allbee, he knows enough of anti-Semitism to be aware that suffering does not have to be inflicted intentionally; and when Allbee says that Leventhal wanted revenge for an anti-Semitic remark which Allbee had made at a party, Leventhal is unable to dismiss that possibility. As Allbee later points out, Leventhal believes that "God doesn't make mistakes. He's the department of weights and measures." Jonathon Baumbach, in his very perceptive analysis of *The Victim*, says that "Leventhal, a victim of real and imaginary persecution, feels guilty because he believes that his suffering, like all suffering, is deserved, yet he cannot

5. Allbee had left a note in Leventhal's mailbox, saying that "Kirby A." would be in the park at nine. Leventhal, who had not seen the note, is unusually restless and decides to walk in the park. His greeting, "Oh, Allbee, isn't it? Allbee?" shows that Leventhal probably did not remember Allbee's first name and probably could not have associated him with the Kirby A. of the note. And the cautious Leventhal probably would not have gone to the park, but would have regarded the note as the work of a prankster or a hoodlum.

But Allbee interprets Leventhal's appearance as an admission of guilt and remorse (when in fact Leventhal has never associated Allbee's dismissal with his own interview with Allbee's employer). Allbee probably left the note because he was unsure of Leventhal; if Leventhal still hated him, then a confrontation would do no good and could only add to Allbee's humiliation.

Improbable in a mathematical sense, the meeting between Allbee and Leventhal is psychologically almost inevitable.

recognize his own mortal sin." [6] It is Leventhal's need to
identify that sin which forces him to listen to Allbee's accusations, and the need to expiate it which moves him to shelter
Allbee and to try to rehabilitate him.

Compelled to help Allbee, Leventhal is compelled also to
find some rational justification for that help. In the search for
"facts" he talks to Williston, who had known of the incident
with Allbee's employer. Jonathon Baumbach points out that
". . . as Leventhal becomes more obsessed with being persecuted he becomes correspondingly more guilt-ridden. Leventhal's behavior toward . . . Williston curiously parallels
Allbee's toward Leventhal. . . . Though the explanations
Leventhal wrests from Williston are painful to him, he compulsively provokes them, a fascinated spectator at his own
execution." [7] Williston informs Leventhal that Allbee had not
been drinking for some time prior to his dismissal and that,
from the employer's point of view, it was quite plausible that
Leventhal had been sent by Allbee to insult him. Furthermore, Williston feels that Leventhal is morally obligated to
help Allbee, and gives him ten dollars (apparently the value
which he places on his own responsibility) to help out. For
the first time Leventhal consciously questions his own motives: "Had he unknowingly . . . wanted to get back at
Allbee?"

Leventhal's realization leads him to admit to Allbee that
there is some justice in his claims: ". . . I'm letting you sleep
here tonight to return a favor, and that's all." But once
acknowledged, the claims grow more insistent and encompass-
ing, until Leventhal returns to the apartment to find himself
locked out and his own bed defiled by Allbee and a whore.
Enraged, he throws them out, though afterward he feels guilty
once again. But Allbee's ultimate claim upon him comes later
that night, when Leventhal awakes to find gas pouring through
the apartment and Allbee with his head in the kitchen stove.

6. Jonathon Baumbach, *The Landscape of Nightmare: Studies in the Contemporary American Novel* (New York: New York University Press, 1965), p. 51.
7. *Ibid.*, p. 50.

" 'You want to murder me? Murder?' Leventhal gasped. . . .
'Me, myself!' Allbee whispered despairingly, as if with his last
breath. 'Me. . . !' " After a brief struggle, Allbee vanishes into
the night, and Leventhal does not pursue him.

The two men do not meet again until the evening in the
theater, several years later. Leventhal now has a better job,
Mary is pregnant, and they have moved to a better section
of Manhattan. Psychologically he is changed too: "Something
recalcitrant seemed to have left him . . . he lost the feeling
that he had, as he used to say, 'got away with it,' his guilty
relief, and the accompanying sense of infringement." He had
never tried to find out what had happened to Allbee, though
he had heard rumors from time to time, and "did not care to
think too much or too literally about it."

Allbee, now a gigolo to a faded movie star, seeks Leventhal
out during the intermission and apologizes for the suicide
attempt: "When you turn against yourself, nobody else means
anything to you either." Allbee begins to tell him that he owes
him something, but Leventhal, reluctant as ever to become
involved, changes the subject. Allbee then says that he has
come to terms with life:

"I'm not the type that runs things. I never could be. I realized that
long ago. I'm the type that comes to terms with whoever runs
things. What do I care? The world wasn't made exactly for me.
What am I going to do about it?"
"What?" Leventhal smiled at him.
"Approximately made for me will have to be good enough. All
that stiffness of once upon a time, that's gone, that's gone." . . . .
"Anyway, I'm enjoying life." Suddenly he looked around and
said, "Say, I've got to run. Yvonne will send them out looking for
me."
"Wait a minute, what's your idea of who runs things?" said
Leventhal. But he heard Mary's voice at his back. Allbee ran in
and sprang up the stairs. The bell continued its dinning, and
Leventhal and Mary were still in the aisle when the houselights
went off. An usher showed them to their seats.

On this seemingly inconclusive note the novel ends.

But the "curtain bell," with its suggestion of death, and the
usher who shows Leventhal to his seat take us back to an

earlier passage in the epilogue, in which Leventhal had been thinking of the contingency of life: "It was a shuffle, all, all accidental and haphazard." His former feeling that he had got away with something had been based on the idea that each of us is somehow assigned a given place, a reserved seat in the theater of life. "But no, this was incorrect. The reality was different. For why should tickets, mere tickets, be promised . . . ? There were more important things to be promised. Possibly there was a promise, since so many felt it. He himself was almost ready to affirm that there was. But it was misunderstood."

Although Bellow leaves the interrelated problems of fate and responsibility unresolved, *The Victim* is a very powerful and complex illumination of them. He shows that they are insoluble not only because man's knowledge and intellectual powers are too limited to deal with their complexity, but also because the problems themselves are multidimensional; they have dimensions which are not accessible to reason. As Bellow tells us later in *Herzog*, the soul lives in more elements than we can ever know. Initiation into these elements is the central theme of his fiction: his heroes are initiated into a larger, transcendental conception of humanity—transcendental in the sense that it transcends the limited, and limiting, dimension of "pure reason."

In *The Victim*, Bellow's spokesman for this conception of humanity is Schlossberg, the old Yiddish journalist whose name ("castlemountain" in German) may be intended to suggest the regality and elevation of his view of life. "More than human," he says, "can you have any use for life? Less than human you don't either." He means that to be more than human (*i.e.*, above human joy and suffering) or less than human (*i.e.*, incapable of feeling joy or suffering) is to be divorced from the deepest reality. The only meaning of life is what we give it, Schlossberg says, so "why be measly? . . . Choose dignity. Nobody knows enough to turn it down." Finally, he says, we must accept human finitude. The old Jewish custom of sewing one's own shroud was a good one because "At least they knew where they stood and who they were, in those days." But at funerals today there is paper grass to hide the dust to which we all return, and "paper grass in the grave makes all the grass paper," Schlossberg says. We pretend that we have eternal life because we don't know what to do with the one we have.

Leventhal, less articulate than Schlossberg, has something of the same instinctive feeling for humanity. On the night when he first allows Allbee to stay in the apartment, Leventhal awakes from a frustrating dream with a strange feeling of "great lucidity," convinced that "everything, everything without exception, took place as if within a single soul or person." And though he knows that "tomorrow this would be untenable," his happiness is undiminished, and he thinks of Schlossberg's words about the marvelous simplicity of life, and of "the explicit recognition in Allbee's eyes which he could not doubt was the double of something in his own." Leventhal has unconsciously accepted Allbee as his double, and in doing so has confirmed his own humanity.

In trying to reject Allbee's claims upon him, in trying to ignore the reality of Allbee's suffering by impugning his motives, Leventhal had been diminishing himself as well. One night he overhears a bitter quarrel on the street below his apartment, and the brief moment of unexplained violence haunts him with "the feeling that he really did not know what went on about him, what strange things, savage things." And when he remembers the look on the face of Allbee's whore, he realizes that "He was wrong about the woman's expression; he was trying to transform it into something he could bear. The truth was probably something far different. . . . Both of them, Allbee and the woman, moved or swam toward him out of a depth of life in which he himself would be lost, choked, ended. There lay horror, evil, all that he had kept himself from." Leventhal had a similar revelation of the depth of life when Mickey died. After his return from the funeral he has a sense of the reality of hell; the crowds in which he moves suggest the "innumerable millions, crossing, touching, pressing. What was that story he had read about Hell cracking open on account of the rage of the god of the sea, and all those souls, crammed together, looking out?" [8] Mickey's death, Allbee's troubles, and the whole sum of Leventhal's own experience have revealed to him that there is no department of weights and measures, that we are all human, all victims.

Yet in a world where contingency is an undeniable fact, where, as Allbee says, "*If* swings us around by the ears like rabbits," man is still confronted with choices. Leventhal asks himself "how could anyone say he was sure? How could he know all that he needed to know in order to say it?" He can't. *If* is inescapable in the factual world of Allbee. But that is not the only world we have. Our choices are made in another world too, the more amorphous, but no less real, qualitative dimension in which Schlossberg can say, "Choose dignity." Even Allbee acknowledges this dimension when he says "I know what really goes on inside me. . . . There isn't a man who doesn't. All this business, 'Know thyself'! Everybody knows but nobody wants to admit." It is in this qualitative dimension that man finds his real freedom, where he is no one's victim but his own.

The Victim is a magnificent achievement. In it the philosophical richness characteristic of all of Bellow's work is given its perfect form. The conception of Allbee (universal being, or Everyman) is brilliant. Entirely believable as a realistic character, he is equally real as the symbolic manifestation of Asa ("healer" or "physician" in Hebrew) Leventhal's darker nature. But it is not a simple allegorical relationship. Ironically, Leventhal as Jew is dark and Allbee as gentile is light, and there are flaws in Leventhal's goodness and in Allbee's evil. The moral overtones and reverberations of the novel seem to be inexhaustible. In trying to heal Allbee, the clumsy physician heals himself, though only partially. Though his ex-

8. The passage which Leventhal is referring to is probably the one from DeQuincey's *The Pains of Opium* which Bellow uses as the second epigraph to *The Victim:*

"Be that as it may, now it was that upon the rocking waters of the ocean the human face began to reveal itself; the sea appeared paved with innumerable faces, upturned to the heavens; faces, imploring, wrathful, despairing; faces that surged upward by thousands, by myriads, by generations. . . ."

periences with Allbee have given him a larger view of
humanity, it is still not large enough; his final conversation
with Allbee is still guarded. And though he saves Allbee's
life, he cannot save his soul; only Allbee himself could do that,
and when we last see him he radiates decay, a death in life.

The structure of the book is also impressive. Because of the
double role of Allbee as realistic character and as projection of
Leventhal's consciousness, Bellow was faced with the problem
of making *The Victim* convincing at both the realistic and
symbolic levels. He merges the two so successfully that the
novel may be read either as realism (as most casual readers
see it) or as symbolism (as many critics see it) without
reference to the other level; yet each level is powerfully
strengthened, and in no way twisted, by the other. For
example, the reader who wants realism is convinced by the
first encounter of Leventhal and Allbee in the park because
the chain of circumstances, though complex, is entirely
probable; the reader who wants symbolism is convinced because Allbee's materialization at that point is psychologically
necessary. Bellow's economy and control in the book are
masterful; they enhance rather than limit its richness.

Finally, *The Victim* achieves, to an extent approached in
Bellow's work only by the shorter *Seize the Day*, an overwhelming reality and relevance as a vision of life. Needless to
say, this is a difficult effect to define. It is not necessarily
realism; *The Scarlet Letter* has it. It is not necessarily
philosophical or moral complexity; *A Farewell to Arms* has it,
despite Holden Caulfield's demur. It is a unique vision of life,
so rich and so subjectively true and coherent that whatever
we "think" of it, we find it deeply moving, permanently interesting, and analytically inexhaustible.

The opening chapters of *The Adventures of Augie March*
(1953) establish a world which is similar, at first glance, to
that of Bellow's earlier fiction. In the first paragraph we learn
that the setting is "Chicago, that somber city," and that the
hero is a self-styled philosopher—he quotes Heraclitus: a
man's character is his fate. He lives in a shabby neighborhood,
and he is Jewish, not because of his own beliefs but because

he is identified and persecuted as a Jew by the neighborhood gangs. It is a world, we soon learn, which is intolerant of differences and cruel to the weak and unfortunate.

But the similarities to Bellow's earlier work are soon overshadowed by the differences. Augie March, though sensitive and intelligent, is not a victim in the sense that Leventhal was: he is not haunted by guilt or even much hurt (beyond the bloody noses, etc., inflicted by young gentiles) by anti-Semitism, and he is not suspicious of other people even when he has grounds for it. There is an openness about Augie which Joseph and Leventhal did not have; this openness defines the world of the novel itself. The other characters in *Augie* are not obtuse reflections of the hero, as those in *Dangling Man* and *The Victim* had been, but living, individual personalities in their own right. Augie, unlike Joseph and Leventhal, is able to accept people as they really are; he does not need to transform them, in Leventhal's words, "into something he could bear."

The reality of the characters is not just a function of Augie's conception of them. The characters in the early Chicago chapters of the novel are created with all the nostalgic love of the narrator—and of the author too, we suspect. They come alive as none of Bellow's other subordinate characters do, and through them he creates a sense of the reality of Chicago in the 1920's and early 1930's which approaches that of the definitive document on that time and place: the Danny O'Neill novels of James T. Farrell.

The Chicago of Augie's boyhood in the 1920's, despite its obvious public and private corruption, is still not the Chicago or New York of the 1940's in Bellow's earlier novels; accustomed to the depravity of men, it had not yet been instructed in the depravity of man. The immigrant families in Augie's neighborhood still see the world and the future of their children through the eyes of essential innocence, unclouded by existential experience.

But the neighborhood—and later Chicago, the nation, and finally the Western hemisphere—is too small to hold Augie. His own expansiveness and his refusal to "lead a disappointed life" carry him through the series of adventures which forms the structure of the novel. These adventures are the typical initiations of the picaresque hero: he drifts in and out of love affairs, friendships, jobs, political and social groups—all of which proffer a fate to him. But none of these fates is good enough; they all threaten imprisonment within some overly restrictive view of life.

Augie's search for a good enough fate is the theme of the novel and the motive for his rejection of the restrictive fates which many of the characters offer him. In rejecting Cousin Anna Coblin's plans for him, he says, "My mind was already dwelling on a good enough fate." He refuses to be adopted by the Renlings because "it wasn't a fate good enough for me." He says that in his quarrel with Thea "I tried to tell her that I had looked all my life for the right thing to do, for a fate good enough, that I had opposed people in what they wanted to make of me. . . ." And he refuses to follow his brother Simon into the worship of money and power because "I had to have a fate good enough, and . . . this came first."

Simon had married for money, hoping to achieve the security and luxury and power which his environment had denied him. But Augie sees that means can become ends, that when man will do anything to survive, "what curious forms he ends up surviving in, becoming them in the process." This is what has happened to Simon. On the other hand, Manny Padilla, Augie's friend who steals books to finance his education and who teaches Augie the tricks of his trade, does not make Simon's mistake: "I don't have larceny in my heart," Manny says, "I'm not a real crook. I'm not interested in it, so nobody can make a fate of it for me. That's not my fate. I might get into a little trouble, but I would never let them make it *my* trouble, get it?"

Fate, then, is of two kinds: the kind we choose and the kind which is chosen for us. Though Augie is not sure of the difference between the two kinds, he chooses to choose. And old Schlossberg of *The Victim* would have admired his choices, for the "fate good enough" is synonymous with Schlossberg's idea of full humanity: in the face of ultimate uncertainty and of all inherent limitations, to accept them, and to choose dignity. Other characters in *Augie* would not meet Schlossberg's standards. Simon becomes less than human; he first hardens himself to human suffering and finally inflicts it simply for pleasure and a sense of power. Thea Fenchel, who carries Augie off to Mexico, tries to be more than human; she feels that "there must be something better than what people call reality," and has only contempt for "faulty humanity," including Augie when he fails her. Thea, Simon, and all the others who try to transform reality into something they can bear, become less than human.

The meaning of *human* is also shrinking because of the increasing abstraction and specialization of modern life. Augie says that "In the world of today your individual man has to be willing to illustrate a more and more narrow and restricted point of existence. And I am not a specialist." The technological revolution has expanded man's knowledge, but increased his awareness of his ignorance perhaps even more dramatically. Augie, seeking the whole meaning of life, finds only specialized interpretations of it. In the technological world man is seen in terms of function. It is an attitude which Augie deplores:

Guys may very likely think, Why hell! What's this talk about fates? and will feel it all comes to me from another day, and a mistaken day, when there were fewer people in the world and there was more room between them so that they grew not like wild grass but like trees in a park, well set apart and developing year by year in the rosy light. Now instead of such comparison you think, Let's see it instead not even as the grass but as a band of particles, a universal shawl of them, and these particles may have functions but certainly lack fates. And there's even an attitude of mind which finds it almost disgusting to be a person and not a function. Nevertheless I stand by my idea of a fate. For which a function is a substitution of a deeper despair.

Societies based upon a concept of man as a function cannot tolerate the search for a worthwhile fate. During the war Augie joins the merchant marine to forestall the possibility of such a universal society. He knows that if the totalitarian view prevails, "where there once had been men like gods there would be nothing but this bug-humanity that would make itself as weird as the threatening universe outside and would imitate it by creating human mechanical regularity as invariable as physical laws. Obedience would be God and freedom the Devil." In America Augie has seen men like his brother Simon become faceless functions of the social structure, but the choice has been theirs. To accept such a deformation is to become anonymous, less than human.

Augie himself refuses to see people as functions, or to merely use them. Simon advises him, for example, to seduce Lucy Magnus so that she will have to marry him and share her inheritance with him. Augie likes her and would enjoy an affair with her, and Lucy would have agreed had he asked; but he says, "I didn't mount the step of power. I could have done so from love, but not to get to the objective." He persists in seeing people as people, and as intrinsically worthwhile because of the essential purity of their deepest desires. He believes in the ultimate goodness of human motives, however grotesque and perverted human behavior may seem. He is an incorrigible idealist. He cites Marx and Rousseau,

this sheer horse's ass of a Jean-Jacques who couldn't get on with a single human being, goes away to the woods of Montmorency, in order to think and write of the *best* government or the *best* system of education. And similarly Marx, with his fierce carbuncles and his poverty and the death of children, whose thought was that the angel of history would try in vain to fly against the wind from the past. And I can mention many others, less great, but however worried, spoiled, or perverse, still wanting to set themselves apart for great ends, and believing in at least one worthiness.

Because he is open and trusting, Augie is vulnerable, "susceptible," he says. He inherited the trait from his mother, "the easy mark of whoever was our father"; and it makes him prey for the schemes of Grandma Lausch, Anna Coblin, Einhorn, Mrs. Renling, Simon, Thea, Sophie Geratis, and many others. After his ship is torpedoed and his naive trust in Bateshaw, his companion in the lifeboat, almost costs him his life, he says, "I took an oath of unsusceptibility." But he doesn't keep it; it would inhibit the search for a worthwhile fate. Augie remains in *opposition,* as Einhorn calls it, but his opposition is open and always susceptible.

Although he distrusts the theories of other people, Augie has a few of his own. One is the notion that everyone has a "chosen thing." Thea's is to become more than human, Mintouchian's is secrecy, Mimi Villars' is "wild appetite," etc. Augie himself has a chosen thing: he "wanted simplicity and denied complexity." It guides his search for the worthwhile fate. Manny Padilla, studying for a math quiz, tells him that "Either this stuff comes easy or it doesn't come at all," and the words are a revelation to Augie: "Of course! Easily or not at all. People were mad to be knocking themselves out over difficulties because they thought difficulty was a sign of the right thing." Augie's longing for simplicity, his feeling that truth must come easily or not at all, is the basis for his famous philosophy of the "axial lines of life":

I have a feeling about the axial lines of life, with respect to which you must be straight or else your existence is merely clownery, hiding tragedy. I must have had a feeling since I was a kid about these axial lines which made me want to have my existence on them, and so I have said "no" like a stubborn fellow to all my persuaders, just on the obstinacy of the memory of these lines, never entirely clear. But lately I have felt these thrilling lines again. When striving stops, there they are as a gift. . . . Truth, love, peace, bounty, usefulness, harmony! . . . And I believe that any man at any time can come back to these axial lines, even if an unfortunate bastard, if he will be quiet and wait it out. . . . At any time life can come together again and man be regenerated . . . the man himself, finite and taped as he is, can still come where the axial lines are. He will be brought into focus. He will live with true joy. Even his pains will be joy if they are true, even his helplessness will not take away his power, even wandering will not take him away from himself, even the big social jokes and hoaxes need not make him ridiculous, even disappointment after disappointment need not take away his love. Death will not be terrible to him if life is not. The embrace of other true people will take away his dread of fast change and short life.

Some critics have regarded the axial lines as the central "message" of the novel. And they are important. But the real

nature of the revelation about the axial lines is made clear at
the beginning of the final chapter:

> I said when I started to make the record that I would be plain
> and heed the knocks as they came, and also that a man's character
> was his fate. Well, then, it's obvious that this fate, or what he
> settles for, is also his character. And since I never have had any
> place of rest, it should follow that I have trouble being still, and
> furthermore my hope is based upon getting to be still so that the
> axial lines can be found. When striving stops, the truth comes as a
> gift—bounty, harmony, love, and so forth. Maybe I can't take these
> very things I want.

The point is that striving never stops, that Augie's hope of
"getting to be still so that the axial lines can be found" is
illusory. We are "still" only in death. The lines themselves do
exist, but only in our minds as ideals, not in the real world.
To achieve them we would have to be more than human.

What is more significant in this passage is the return to
Heraclitus, for the story has now proved what at the beginning
had been only an assertion: that a man's character is his fate.
Mintouchian, who seems to have the role in *Augie* which
Schlossberg had in *The Victim*, tells Augie that "you are the
author of your death. What is the weapon? The hammer and
nails of your character."

Character is expressed through choice, and choices must be
made in the context of the human condition. Augie has learned
that "there is a darkness. It is for everyone. You don't, as
some perhaps imagine, try it, one foot into it like a barber-
shop 'September Morn.' Nor are lowered into it with visitor's
curiosity. . . . Nor are lifted straight out after an unlucky
tumble. . . . Only some Greeks and admirers of theirs, in
their liquid noon, where the friendship of beauty to human
things was perfect, thought they were clearly divided from
this darkness. And these Greeks too were in it." It is in this
darkness that choices must always be made. It is a universal
darkness, and we are plunged into it above our heads and
against our wills, and no one is exempt from it. Yet the
means of our salvation, Augie says, are "always superabundantly about and insistently offered to us." The darkness

simply gives significance to the light; suffering gives added dimension (the "depth of life" that Leventhal discovered) and added significance to our choices. "Even the Son of Man," says Mintouchian, "made it hard so He would have enough in common with our race to be its God."

At the time of its publication, *Augie* seemed to be a technical breakthrough, the mirror opposite of *The Victim*, which is one of the most convoluted novels in our literature. The transition from it to *Augie* is something like going from the later Henry James to *Huckleberry Finn*. And because of the *opposition* in Augie, "his pursuit of a primal innocence," as Leslie Fiedler puts it,[9] and the episodic structure of his story, comparisons with Huck were inevitable. Augie, whose adventures won the National Book Award for Bellow, was seen as the picaresque *schlimazl,* a Jewish Huck Finn whose "failures are not only accidental; they are in a sense *designed* as a commentary on the successful," as Frederick J. Hoffman has said.[10] *Augie* has been the most widely read of Bellow's novels (though *Herzog* is overtaking it) and probably the most influential. Its role in stimulating later work in the vein of Jewish picaresque humor, such as that of Bruce Jay Friedman, is fairly obvious; and in some ways *Augie* seems prophetic even of such books as Joseph Heller's *Catch–22* and John Barth's *The Sot-Weed Factor*.

The best part of *Augie*, however, is the least picaresque: the early chapters dealing with the boyhood in Chicago. In these chapters Bellow achieves a sense of life which the later, more expansive chapters dissipate. The novel is, as Jonathon Baumbach remarks, "over extended." [11] Or as Leslie Fiedler puts it, "*Augie,* which begins with such rightness, such conviction, does not know how to end; shriller and shriller, wilder and wilder, it finally whirls apart in a frenzy of fake euphoria

9. Leslie Fiedler, "Saul Bellow," in Richard Kostelanetz (ed.), *On Contemporary Literature* (New York: Avon, 1964), p. 291.
10. Frederick J. Hoffman, "The Fool of Experience: Saul Bellow's Fiction," in Harrry T. Moore (ed.), *Contemporary American Novelists* (Carbondale: Southern Illinois University Press, 1964), p. 91.
11. Baumbach, *The Landscape of Nightmare*, p. 36.

and exclamatory prose." [12] At least part of this effect, however, is intentional; Bellow is aware of the desperation of Augie's search and of the fakery of his euphoria, to some extent, at least. And he makes Augie himself aware of it, as we have seen in the final passage about the axial lines. Still, one could say of *Augie* what Dr. Johnson said of *Paradise Lost:* we would not wish it longer than it is.

Although *Augie* represents a dramatic reversal in Bellow's technique, it is a much easier achievement than *The Victim.* The unifying principle of the novel is Augie's search for a worthwhile fate, and though the first-person narrative gives immediacy to that search, it lacks the objective complexity of the narration of *The Victim.* Augie's character is shown in his relationships with the other characters, and is explained by Augie himself. While there are certain differences in the two views, they are essentially the same. *Augie* lacks the dramatic irony of *Huckleberry Finn,* in which the author's view of the hero is always clearly larger than the hero's own view, and where much of the reader's pleasure comes from the awareness of this difference. In *Augie* there is less for the reader to discover than in *The Victim,* and much more for him to listen to. Despite the informal, idiomatic, often delightful way in which Augie tells his story, it has an underlying pedagogic tone which becomes increasingly obtrusive and annoying as the story goes on. Augie, so distrustful of theories, finally becomes a theoretician himself. In *Herzog* Bellow has his hero realize this irony; and Bellow himself may have realized it in *Augie,* but that possibility does not add much interest to the theorizing itself, which becomes almost constant in the later chapters. In *Henderson the Rain King* the lectures are shorter and more controlled; and they are objectified in the brilliant conception of the incidents themselves. But though *Augie* is archetypal in a sense, too, the story itself is so explicit that the explicit theorizing only weighs it down. Toward the end of *Augie,* and in *Herzog,* the reader

12. Fiedler, "Saul Bellow," p. 292.

wants to echo Augie's own complaint: "Why did I always have to fall among theoreticians!"

From the expansive style of *Augie* Bellow returned to his earlier, tightly controlled technique for *Seize the Day* (1956), the shortest of his novels. In it he recreates the claustral atmosphere of *The Victim.* The protagonist, Tommy Wilhelm, is paralyzed by his remembrance of things past and by his anxieties for the future. As a result, he is helpless in the here-and-now. His life is a case history of failure. He had left college in his sophomore year to go to Hollywood, against the evidence of an unsuccessful screen test, against the wishes of his parents, and against the advice of a talent scout whose most important clients, it turned out, were whores. After seven wasted years there, he had felt that it was too late to enter a profession (though his father, a very successful physician, would have paid for a medical education), and had become a salesman of playground equipment. With an income in the 32 per cent tax bracket, the promise of promotion to an executive position, and a mistress in Albany, Wilhelm seemed to have arrived. But when the president of the corporation filled the executive position with a young relative, Wilhelm quit in indignation. Now he is living in New York's Hotel Gloriana, whose guests are primarily the retired and superfluous, and he is going through the motions of finding another position.

The events of the day shown in the novel make it clear that he is only temporizing. Faced with bitter demands by his wife, whom he had deserted, for the support of his family (they have two sons), he tries to borrow from his father and nervously watches his savings disappear in the commodities market.

Dr. Adler, Wilhelm's father, is a selfish and vain old man of eighty who leads a dull and circumspect life in the Hotel Gloriana. While he boasts to his friends of Wilhelm's success as a salesman, he refuses to become involved in his failures. When Wilhelm asks for help, his father responds only with gratuitous advice. Accustomed to deference and flattery from generations of his medical students and from his aged friends in the hotel, Dr. Adler is angry and resentful when Tommy's pathetic pleas for help expose the father's selfishness.

Equally grotesque is Wilhelm's relationship with Dr. Tamkin, who has invested Wilhelm's last seven hundred dollars in the commodities market. Tamkin claims to be a psychologist, and his fantastic stories about his patients are obviously blatant violations of truth as well as of professional ethics. Although Wilhelm recognizes that Tamkin is a charlatan, he needs him, for Tamkin is the only other human being who has any real interest in Wilhelm's problems, even if his motive is exploitation. Tamkin does have real insights and is able to communicate these to Wilhelm despite the latter's suspicions. Tamkin's philosophy fits in remarkably well with what Wilhelm has learned empirically and intuitively over the years.

The grotesque nature of Wilhelm himself and of his relationships with others arises as much from his sensitivity and perceptiveness as from his failures and instabilities. Beneath his bizarre actions and mannerisms there is a basic integrity which is constantly at odds with the dishonesty around him. In fact, his past failures may be due, at least in part, to his refusal to sell out to the world of comfortable appearances. His failure in the movies, for example, may be due partly to his unwillingness to yield himself completely to the make-believe world of Hollywood. He refuses to enter medicine because he has a horror of suffering and of the business of profiting by it. And his sympathy for his family has kept him from evading the shrill demands of his wife. Several times throughout the course of the day his sensitivity betrays him: in his talk with the news dealer, in his arguments with his father, in his reluctance to challenge Tamkin's judgment of the commodity trends, even in his act of sympathy for old Rappaport (Tamkin makes his getaway while Wilhelm guides the old man to the cigar store). As William J. Handy has pointed out in his excellent interpretation of *Seize the Day*, "It is a final irony of the novel that the one person who clings to the reality of what it means to be human is, in the eyes of his world, a misfit. Yet we feel that it is precisely in his possession of a sense of humanity that Tommy Wilhelm does not emerge a defeated man, a pathetic victim of forces beyond his control." [13]

Although Wilhelm has many psychological problems, his deepest problem is philosophical: the mystery of his own relationship to himself, to others, and to the universe. The problems of social success and failure in Seize the Day are the surface reflections of a deeper concern with the ultimate questions.

Wilhelm's greatest desire is for the achievement and recognition of his individuality. His decision to go to Hollywood, made against the advice of everyone and against his own judgment, had been an attempt to find and assert his individuality. So was his change of name, from Wilhelm Adler to Tommy Wilhelm. This had hurt and alienated his father, who persists in calling him Wilky in an attempt to maintain the father-child relationship. The name change was a gesture of defiance, only partially successful, against a world which permits too little freedom:

. . . there's really very little that a man can change at will. He can't change his lungs, or nerves, or constitution or temperament. They're not under his control. When he's young and strong and impulsive and dissatisfied with the way things are he wants to rearrange them to assert his freedom. He can't rearrange the government or be differently born; he only has a little scope and maybe a foreboding, too, that essentially you can't change. Nevertheless, he makes a gesture and becomes Tommy Wilhelm. Wilhelm had always had a great longing to be Tommy. He had never, however, succeeded in feeling like Tommy, and in his soul had always remained Wilky. . . . Yes, it had been a stupid thing to do, but it was his imperfect judgment at the age of twenty which should be blamed. He had cast off his father's name, and with it his father's opinion of him. It was, he knew it was, his bid for liberty, Adler being in his mind the title of the species, Tommy the freedom of the person. But Wilky was his inescapable self.

Wilhelm's whole life has been a series of unsuccessful choices, made almost invariably in the face of reason: "After

13. William J. Handy, "Saul Bellow and the Naturalistic Hero," Texas Studies in Literature and Language, V (1964), 543.

much thought and hesitation and debate he invariably took the course he had rejected innumerable times. Ten such decisions made up the history of his life. He had decided that it would be a bad mistake to go to Hollywood, and then he went. He had made up his mind not to marry his wife, but ran off and got married. He had resolved not to invest money with Tamkin, and then had given him a check."

While these choices have been unsuccessful in a practical sense, they have permitted Wilhelm to achieve and retain some measure of identity. But now, with his money disappearing and the demands of his wife and his creditors growing more insistent, he is faced with the impending surrender of his identity and his destiny. There seems to be no way out. At forty-four he is an obvious failure. He cannot find a job which will pay him what he needs, and he cannot afford to take a job which will pay him less. His speculation in the commodities market is going badly. He does not wish to crawl to the Rojax Corporation, which might not take him back even if he did, or to beg from his father, who might also refuse. In either case, he would repudiate earlier decisions which had shown courage and integrity. In desperation he approaches his father, hoping that the old man's sense of responsibility (not his love, which Wilhelm never had) will overcome his selfishness. But the father responds with preaching rather than help, and the damage to Wilhelm's pride and individuality is as great as if the help had been given.

This trap of circumstances has its parallel in internal conflicts. Psychologically, Wilhelm is trapped between past and future, between the remembrance of failure and the premonition of disaster. His response is evasion of both the past and the future: he goes to considerable trouble both to conceal his failures from the world of the Hotel Gloriana and to avoid leaving that world, which despite its falsity is still more certain than the future. The name of the hotel is appropriate, for its environment is as far removed from reality, at least so far as Wilhelm is concerned, as Spenser's fairyland.

On the philosophical level, which is the most important, *Seize the Day* is perhaps most meaningful if read as a novel of the absurd. Wilhelm is modern man, caught in the classical dilemma of the absurd: the irreconcilable conflict between the human need for unity or rational order in life and the ultimate incomprehensibility of the universe around and within him—in the phrase of Camus, "the constant confrontation between man and his own obscurity." [14] Grotesque and shabby failure that he is, Wilhelm is nevertheless heroic since, despite his psychological defense mechanisms, he has not forsaken his quest for reality. Camus says that "there is no finer sight than that of the intelligence at grips with a reality that transcends it." In his relentless self-examination, then, Wilhelm still retains elements of heroism; he is Camus' philosophical rebel, although the flame of courage is flickering.

Into this crisis in Wilhelm's life comes the charlatan Tamkin, with his fantastic stories and his schemes for a quick killing in grain futures. And although Wilhelm sees him for what he is, he accepts him. Although Tamkin swindles Wilhelm, he enriches him too: " 'With me,' said Dr. Tamkin, 'I am at my most efficient when I don't need the fee. When I only love. Without a financial reward. I remove myself from the social influence. Especially money. The spiritual compensation is what I look for. Bringing people into the here-and-now. The real universe. That's the present moment. Only the present is real—the here-and-now. Seize the day.' " This message, to seize the day, rather than submit to it, is the truth which Wilhelm needs. As Camus puts it, the philosophy of the absurd "challenges the world anew every second." The past is no good to Wilhelm because it is obsolete, a chronicle of failures. The future is unreal also, a nightmare of apprehensions. He must live in the "here-and-now," rather than in regret or anxiety. He must achieve what Camus calls "man's sole dignity: the dogged revolt against his condition, perseverance in an effort considered sterile."

In the remarkable final scene of *Seize the Day*, Wilhelm is in pursuit of Tamkin, whom he thinks he has recognized in

14. Albert Camus, *The Myth of Sisyphus, and Other Essays* (New York: Vintage Books, 1959), p. 40. Quotations from Camus in the subsequent discussion are also from *The Myth of Sisyphus*.

the street. But Wilhelm is trapped in the crowd and swept into a funeral parlor, where he finds himself in the line of viewers at the bier. In the face of the corpse, he sees something which transfixes him and fills him with uncontrollable anguish: "The flowers and lights fused ecstatically in Wilhelm's blind, wet eyes; the heavy sea-like music came up to his ears. It poured into him where he had hidden himself in the center of a crowd by the great and happy oblivion of tears. He heard it and sank deeper than sorrow through torn sobs and cries toward the consummation of his heart's ultimate need."

In the context of the absurd, the ultimate and only universal reality is death. In the face of this anonymous corpse, Wilhelm has seen himself and humanity. The truth "deeper than sorrow" is the recognition of this ultimate reality, man's inevitable fate. In that fate Wilhelm discovers his own humanity. And the "heart's ultimate need" is the acceptance of that truth and a commitment to life in spite of, indeed in defiance of, the lack of any ultimate meaning. Camus' conclusion to *The Myth of Sisyphus* is very close to Tommy Wilhelm's revelation in the funeral parlor: "The absurd man says yes and his effort will henceforth be unceasing. If there is a personal fate, there is no higher destiny, or at least there is but one which he concludes is inevitable and despicable. For the rest, he knows himself to be the master of his days. . . . The struggle itself toward the heights is enough to fill a man's heart. One must imagine Sisyphus happy."

The narrative technique of *Seize the Day* is closer to that of *The Victim* than to Bellow's other novels. Although the narrative enters the mind of Dr. Adler for a few moments, Wilhelm's point of view entirely dominates the novel. Wilhelm is both expansive and withdrawn. Like Augie, he is an open personality. "I am an idiot. I have no reserve," he says. He is compulsively gregarious, trusting, and confiding. But, like Leventhal, he is tortured by guilt and insecurity which somewhat undercuts his natural trust and confidence in others. He is another dangling man, with a deep need to believe in himself, in others, and in life, but with an equally strong compulsion to deny that belief because it seems so little justified by what he has experienced. He is suspended between the hope that he is choosing and the dread that he has been chosen. Like all of Bellow's heroes, Wilhelm has a sensitivity which overruns his ability to articulate it.

Tamkin, on the other hand, articulates far beyond his perceptions. In the real world he is an unscrupulous con man, full of grab-bag theories and wild talk, and hopelessly inept in the marketplace which he exalts—literally a dirty, stinking cheat. But like Allbee of *The Victim*, he has another function. In the world of Wilhelm's imagination he is the salvation which, as Augie had said, is "always superabundantly about and insistently offered to us." In the grotesque junk yard of his mind Tamkin somehow finds, and sells for Wilhelm's last seven hundred dollars, exactly what Wilhelm needs to get going again. The polar opposition of their characters is a polar attraction too, and the strange ways in which such different beings can fulfill each other's needs is a major revelation of the novel—and of Bellow's work as a whole.

In *Seize the Day,* as in much of the other work, the characters move in a double dimension. The Gloriana is both an oppressive, imprisoning reality and a strange, unreal dream; and Wilhelm lives in both at once, with past and future looming in and out of focus in the strangeness of the here-and-now. It is Leventhal's vision of hell cracked open and the innumerable souls staring out, but now materialized, peopled with Wilhelm and Tamkin and Dr. Adler and the others.

And perhaps the strangest thing about it is that it is comic; page for page *Seize the Day* is Bellow's richest comic achievement. The comedy lies not so much in the idiosyncrasies of the characters, or in the startling things they say, or in their incongruous and ridiculous situations, as in a merging of all of these in a rich, coherent criticism of life. The comedy persists until the very last paragraph:

He, alone of all the people in the chapel, was sobbing. No one knew who he was.
One woman said, "Is that perhaps the cousin from New Orleans they were expecting?"

"It must be somebody real close to carry on so."

"Oh my, oh my! To be mourned like that," said one man and looked at Wilhelm's heavy shaken shoulders, his clutched face and whitened fair hair, with wide, glinting, jealous eyes.

"The man's brother, maybe?"

"Oh, I doubt that very much," said another bystander. "They're not alike at all. Night and day."

The ultimate irony of this dark comedy is, of course, that Wilhelm *is* the man's brother, that they *are* alike; and in the last paragraph, which itself is darkly comic, Wilhelm sinks "deeper than sorrow" to this tragic realization which will be "the consummation of his heart's ultimate need." The last paragraph achieves its moving revelation because of the comedy which precedes it. Wilhelm's realization is the climax of that comedy, the inevitable event to which it all leads, and its fulfillment. In fulfilling the comedy it also transcends it, and the novel ends in that lonely region where comedy and tragedy finally merge in perfect artistic truth.

The revelation of the final scene of *Seize the Day* becomes the central theme of Bellow's next novel, *Henderson the Rain King* (1959). In twentieth-century America, Henderson says, our greatest problem is "to encounter death." This encounter and its meaning become the focal point of Henderson's story.

Gene Henderson is a huge man, and his appetites match his size. As the name Eugene implies, he is "of noble race": "his great-grandfather was Secretary of State, his great-uncles were ambassadors to England and France, and his father was the famous scholar Willard Henderson who wrote that book on the Albigensians, a friend of William James and Henry Adams." His father's fortune of three million dollars has enabled Henderson to choose the kind of life he wants to lead.

His choice is an unusual one for a millionaire, and an offensive one to his neighbors. He raises pigs on the two-hundred-year-old Henderson estate. "I took," he says,

all the handsome old farm buildings, the carriage house with panelled stalls—in the old days a rich man's horses were handled like opera singers—and the fine old barn with the belvedere above the hayloft, a beautiful piece of architecture, and I filled them up with pigs, a pig kingdom, with pig houses on the lawn and in the flower garden. The greenhouse too—I let them root out the old bulbs. Statues from Florence and Salzburg were turned over. The place stank of swill and pigs and the mashes cooking, and dung.

Henderson's vocation reflects his concern with death and his attitude toward life in general: "The dead are my boarders, eating me out of house and home. The hogs were my defiance. I was telling the world that it was a pig." The decision had been made during the war, in which Henderson, an infantry captain and one of only two survivors of his original unit, had seen the senseless destruction of Monte Cassino and the death of many of the finest men of his generation. He himself had been severely wounded by a land mine.

The decision is also a humbling one; he speaks of it several times in connection with Daniel's prophecy to Nebuchadnezzar: ". . . they shall drive thee from men, and thy dwelling shall be with the beasts of the field, and they shall make thee to eat grass as oxen, and they shall wet thee with the dew of heaven, and seven times shall pass over thee, till thou know that the most High ruleth in the kingdom of men, and giveth it to whomsoever he will." [15]

It is a confrontation with death which drives Henderson to Africa. His life with his second wife, Lily, is falling apart. While he is shouting at her in a violent quarrel, their old housekeeper, Miss Lenox, dies of a heart attack in the kitchen. He decides that, for everyone's sake, he must leave. He says, "I suppose some people are more full of death than others.

---

15. Daniel 5:25 (King James version). Daniel's prophecy is fulfilled, and King Nebuchadnezzar acknowledges the omnipotence of God. In Chapter 2 of Daniel the King had threatened Daniel with death if he could not interpret a dream, which the King himself had forgotten. This dream, like the later one, involved the transitory nature of Nebuchadnezzar's kingdom in comparison to God's. Daniel's ability to recall the dream, given to him by God, established him as the leading prophet of the King's court. Nebuchadnezzar's son Belshazzar was slain by the Medes and Persians. It was Darius the Mede who cast Daniel into the den of lions. Daniel's survival convinced Darius of the power of Daniel's God. Henderson's adventure in the lion's den may have been suggested by Daniel, Chapter 6.

Evidently I happen to have a great death potential." King Dahfu of the Wariri recognizes this as the real reason for Henderson's flight into Africa: "You fled what you were. You did not believe you had to perish. Once more, and a last time, you tried the world. With a hope of alteration."

At the age of fifty-five Henderson feels that life, as well as death, is closing in on him: "the facts begin to crowd me and soon I get a pressure in the chest. A disorderly rush begins— my parents, my wives, my girls, my children, my farm, my animals, my habits, my money, my music lessons, my drunkenness, my prejudices, my brutality, my teeth, my face, my soul! I have to cry, "No, no, get back, curse you, let me alone!" And they pile into me from all sides. It turns into chaos." This is a familiar feeling to Henderson, the feeling of strangulation by the many tentacles of his own existence. He had had the same feeling at the end of a wild tour of Europe with Lily during his marriage to his first wife, Frances; it occurred when he had seen an octopus beckoning through the glass in a marine aquarium in the south of France and had been chilled with a sense of "a cosmic coldness in which I felt I was dying. The tentacles throbbed and motioned through the glass, the bubbles sped upward, and I thought, 'This is my last day. Death is giving me notice.'"

Henderson is caught in the familiar existential dilemma of Bellow's heroes: yearning for order and meaning in his life, he finds only chaos and meaninglessness. He feels helpless, trapped by two inescapable facts of life. The first, as we have seen, is death. The second is man's inability to know reality when he sees it. "We are funny creatures," Henderson says. "We don't see the stars as they are, so why do we love them? They are not small gold objects but endless fire. *Strange? Why shouldn't it be strange? It is strange. It is all strange.*" For Henderson "reality has no fixed dwelling"; it is a product of time and circumstances and, especially, personalities: "The world of facts is real, all right, and not to be altered. The physical is all there, and it belongs to science. But then there is the noumenal department, and there we create and create and create. As we tread our overanxious ways, we think we know what is real. And I was telling the truth to Lily after a fashion. I knew it better, all right, but I knew it because it was mine—filled, flowing, and floating with my own resemblances; as hers was with *her* resemblances. Oh, what a revelation!"

Because reality is always beyond his grasp, man feels alienated from the world, from others, and from himself. He will always be a stranger to his fellow travelers on this journey to death: "This planet has billions of passengers on it, and these were preceded by infinite billions and there are vaster billions to come, and none of these, no, not one, can I hope ever to understand. Never!" The fluid nature of modern society deepens this sense of alienation. "Nobody truly occupies a station in life any more," says Henderson. "There are displaced persons everywhere."

Henderson has arrived at a confrontation with the absurd, as Camus defines it, at the "last crossroad where thought hesitates." In the primitive civilization of Africa he hopes to find certain fundamental values which have been submerged by his own. There is a voice within him which cries out "I want, I want, I want." He does not understand the nature of the imprisoned want, and all of his attempts to appease the voice fail. It is only in the lion's den, under the tutelage of King Dahfu, when Henderson tries with everything that is in him to become a lion, that he finally learns what the voice has been saying:

And so I was the beast. I gave myself to it, and all my sorrow came out in the roaring. My lungs supplied the air but the note came from my soul. The roaring scalded my throat and hurt the corners of my mouth and presently I filled the den like a bass organ pipe. This was where my heart had sent me, with its clamor. This is where I ended up. Oh Nebuchadnezzar! How well I understood that prophecy of Daniel. For I had claws, and hair, and some teeth, and I was bursting with hot noise, but when all this had come forth, there was still a remainder. The last thing of all was my human longing.

It is this want, this human longing, which has not been satisfied by the conditions of Henderson's life. The facts began to crowd him and he had to ask the ultimate question: why? King Dahfu of the Wariri, who has evolved a complete system for categorizing psychological types much as a botanist would classify plants, shrewdly places Henderson in the category labelled "Salvation." "*If I couldn't have my soul,*" Henderson thinks, "*it would cost the earth a catastrophe.*"

The destiny of his generation, Henderson believes, is "to go out in the world and try to find the wisdom of life." And the search is not to be purely philosophical; wisdom is to be used as the basis for action. If he had been truly overwhelmed by the chaos and meaninglessness of the world, he might have carried out one of the suicide threats he made from time to time. Instead, like Camus' rebel, he hopes against hope that something can be done. "Why should there be no hope for suffering? It so happens that I believe something can be done," he says. Henderson recognizes that "There is some kind of service motivation which keeps on after me." It is this ambition for service, together with his spiritual dissatisfaction, which leads him eventually to his time of trial among the Wariri.

Henderson's journey into the "prehuman past" takes him first to the Arnewi, a gentle people whose cattle are dying because the Arnewi will not permit them to drink from a cistern which has become populated with frogs. His first act among the Arnewi is to set a bush afire with his cigarette lighter before a group of Arnewi children, an incident which may be a parody of the appearance of God to Moses in a burning bush. Shamed into a wrestling contest with Prince Itelo, Henderson wins. This contest is more symbolic than he realizes; Itelo regards him afterward almost with reverence, and the queen's sister, Mtalba, betrothes herself to him. Failing to persuade the Arnewi that the frogs will not harm their cattle, Henderson plans to annihilate the frogs with an ingenious homemade bomb. Unfortunately, the bomb destroys the cistern too, and Henderson leaves the Arnewi in disgrace.

He and his native guide and companion, Romilayu, then journey to the land of the Wariri (children of darkness,

Romilayu calls them), who are less gentle than the Arnewi. They are captured by the Wariri and spend their first night in the village in a hut where they find a corpse (which, Henderson later learns, is that of the former Rain King). They are taken the next morning to the palace of Dahfu, King of the Wariri and a friend of Itelo. Dahfu had been educated in the Near East and had been close to his M.D. degree when he was summoned back to the tribe by his father's death. Henderson attends a rain ceremony with the King, impulsively performs a feat of strength at which a large native had failed, and finds that he has become the Sungo, or Rain King of the Wariri. Dahfu then begins to take Henderson along on his daily visits to his lion's den.

The Wariri apparently subscribe to the ancient belief that the vitality of their nation depends upon the vitality of their god-king. And that vitality is tested by the sexual demands of his wives. When he fails to meet these demands, the wives report him to the priests, who strangle him, and the kingship passes to the oldest son who is of age. What Henderson does not learn until the death of Dahfu is that if there is no son who is of age, the kingship passes to the Rain King. Upon the death of the king his spirit is assumed to pass into the body of a lion cub, which is chosen and marked by the priests and which the new king must recapture unharmed within two years in order to retain his throne—and his life.

The god-king concept of the Wariri follows closely the concept of an African tribe called the Shilluk, which practiced the ceremonial murder of their king well into the twentieth century. This practice was first reported by Sir James Frazer in *The Golden Bough* and was discussed by Miss Jessie L. Weston in *From Ritual to Romance*. One or both of these accounts [16] may have been Bellow's source for the custom of

---

16. A condensed version of Frazer's account is given in Jessie L. Weston, *From Ritual to Romance* (New York: Peter Smith, 1941):

The Shilluk . . . . are a pastoral people, their wealth consisting in flocks and herds, grain and millet. The King . . . is regarded with extreme reverence, as being a reincarnation of Nyakang, the semi-divine hero who settled the tribe in their present territory. Nyakang is the

the Wariri in *Henderson the Rain King*, though the concept
of the lion seems to have been his own invention, suggested
perhaps by the book of Daniel.

Bellow's interest in these African tribes, however, is more
philosophical than anthropological. From the gentle Arnewi,
Henderson learns of the concept of *grun-tu-molani*, which is
their name for man's great desire to live, and is apparently the
cornerstone of their philosophy. The concept greatly appeals
to him, since it is the analogue to his own fierce determination
not to agree to the death of his soul. He interprets *grun-tu-
molani* to mean that life must not only be preserved, but given
transcendent meaning.

But Henderson's sojourn with the Arnewi is relatively brief.
About two thirds of the book is devoted to his adventures
among the Wariri. In King Dahfu, who has been educated in
the modern world but who has chosen to be a doomed god-
king in a primitive world, Bellow has an equal for Henderson
and a fertile source for philosophical dialogue. Dahfu is
familiar with the Arnewi and their concept of *grun-tu-molani*,
but he says that *grun-tu-molani* is not enough. His own

---

rain-giver, on whom their lives and prosperity depend; there are several
shrines in which sacred Spears, now kept for sacrificial purposes, are
preserved. . . .

The King, though regarded with reverence, must not be allowed to
become old or feeble, lest, with the diminishing vigour of the ruler, the
cattle should sicken, and fail to bear increase, the crops should rot in the
field and men die in ever growing numbers. One of the signs of failing
energy is the King's inability to fulfil the desires of his wives, of whom
he has a large number. When this occurs the wives report the fact to
the chiefs, who condemn the King to death forthwith, communicating the
sentence to him by spreading a white cloth over his face and knees
during his mid-day slumber. Formerly the King was starved to death in
a hut, in company with a young maiden but (in consequence, it is said
of the great vitality and protracted suffering of one King) this is no
longer done; the precise manner of death is difficult to ascertain; Dr.
Seligmann, who was Sir J. G. Frazer's authority, thinks that he is now
strangled in a hut, especially ereceted for that purpose," 55–56.

Another king-who-must-die was discovered by Frazer in Nigeria.
Cautious scholars doubted that candidates would apply for such a
hazardous position, but Miss Weston says that Frazer was correct, and
that "evidence shows clearly that not only does such an office exist, but
that it is by no means an unpopular post," 61.

philosophy, he says, requires something more; and it is at this point that he first takes Henderson into the lion's den.

Dahfu believes above all in the capability of the human mind:

Men of most powerful appetite have always been the ones to doubt reality the most. Those who could not bear that hopes should turn to misery, and loves to hatreds, and deaths and silences, and so on. The mind has a right to its reasonable doubts, and with every short life it awakens and sees and understands what so many other minds of equally short life span have left behind. It is natural to refuse belief that so many small spans should have made glorious one large thing. That human creatures by pondering should be *correct*. This is what makes a fellow gasp.

The human mind, in other words, transcends the limitations of individual human lives. The important fact is not that the mind is limited in perception or destroyed by death, but simply that it is able to reason.

Furthermore, Dahfu believes that the mind is free, that there are no inherent limitations on human thought for the man who has the courage and the strength to follow wherever his intelligence may lead him.

Dahfu believes that every man is a mirror of his mind, that the mind originates and controls all human actions, even that the features of the body are caused only partly by heredity and are influenced by the mind.[17] (Henderson, with his grotesque features and physique, finds this idea less than flattering.) According to Dahfu, everything depends upon the achievement of a proper state of mind: "It is all a matter of having a desirable model in the cortex. For the noble self-conception is everything. For as conception is, so the fellow is. Put differently, you are in the flesh as your soul is."

For Dahfu the full significance of life is to be found not in the future, but in the present moment or, as Tamkin put it in *Seize the Day*, the here-and-now. Henderson recognizes

17. According to Richard G. Stern, "Henderson's Bellow," *Kenyon Review*, XXI (1959), 655–56, 658–61, the novel is influenced by the somatic psychology of Wilhelm Reich. Stern had talked with Bellow during the writing of *Henderson*.

Dahfu as "no mere dreamer but one of those dreamer-doers," and therefore regards him as superior to himself, a "mere dreamer." In several places in the book Henderson identifies himself with another Biblical figure, Joseph the son of Jacob. Joseph was a dreamer and interpreter of dreams, and his brothers were jealous of him and skeptical of his grandiose dreams in which the brothers, the parents, and even the sun, moon, and stars made obeisance to Joseph. Because of their jealousy, the brothers sold him into slavery and showed his blood-stained coat to Jacob, who loved him above all the others. When a Wariri herdsman emerges from the rocks and brush ahead of Henderson and Romilayu on their journey to the land of the Wariri, Henderson thinks immediately of the man who directed Joseph to Dothan, where his brothers waited to cast him into the pit. And indeed the herdsman does direct them into an ambush. Henderson thinks of Joseph again as he enters the arena to witness the rain ceremony, and he recalls the remark made by the brothers, "Behold, this dreamer cometh," as Joseph approached their trap (Genesis 37:19).

Henderson/Joseph, then, is a dreamer, while Dahfu/David is a dreamer-doer. Or to put it another way, Henderson is merely *becoming* while Dahfu has achieved *being*. As Henderson himself explains it, "some people found satisfaction in *being* (Walt Whitman: 'Enough to merely be! Enough to breathe! Joy! Joy! All over joy!'). *Being*. Others were taken up with *becoming*. Being people have all the breaks. Becoming people are very unlucky, always in a tizzy. The Becoming people are always having to make explanations or offer justifications to the Being people. . . . Becoming was beginning to come out of my ears. Enough! Enough! Time to Be! Burst the spirit's sleep." *Being* people live in the present moment, the here-and-now, while *becoming* people endure the present in order to live at some time in the future. The great value of Atti the lioness, Dahfu tells Henderson, is that "she is unavoidable. And that is what you need, as you are an avoider. Oh, you have accomplished momentous avoidances. But she will change that. She will make consciousness to shine. She will burnish you. She will force the present moment upon you."

The key to a meaningful life, according to King Dahfu, is to live in the present moment, the here-and-now, and to use all of the power of the mind to heighten the intensity and meaning of that moment. Such a course is not for the timid. "More of fear than of any other thing has been created," Dahfu says, and he admits the difficulty of overcoming this most pervasive of human emotions. Nevertheless, the conquest is worth any price, even death.

The priceless lesson which Henderson learns from the doomed god-king is the meaning of death and suffering. Henderson's flight to Africa had been a flight from death, not only the death of old Miss Lenox but the inescapable fact of his own death. In learning to face the lion in its den, Henderson also learned to face death—not to face it without fear, perhaps, but to face it without the aid of the countless evasions which civilized man employs. Later he has the opportunity to call upon this experience, when he accompanies Dahfu into the jungle to capture the symbolic lion. "The snarling of this animal was indeed the voice of death," Henderson thinks as he and Dahfu wait for the great male lion-king in the trap. Significantly, after Dahfu has been fatally mauled by the partly trapped lion, it is Henderson, in a state of rage which overcomes his fear, who immobilizes the great beast by tying up the lion's savagely thrusting hindquarters.

He learns that his "scheme for an untroubled but eternal life" has been only an illusion. If there were no suffering and no death, man would not be driven to ask the profound questions which alone can illuminate his existence. "It's too bad," Henderson says, "but suffering is about the only reliable burster of the spirit's sleep." It gives added dimensions to the spiritual life. Henderson wonders sometimes "Does truth come in blows?" Dahfu agrees that there are blows, which only the very strong can absorb without yielding to the temptation to pass them on to others, but he feels that the truth content of the blows is another matter. Nevertheless, Henderson recognizes that "I had no business to make terms with life, but had to accept such conditions as it would let me have." And finally, even death itself may be philosophically justified. After Dahfu's death, Henderson considers that "maybe time was invented so that misery might have an end. So that it shouldn't last forever? There may be something in this. And bliss, just the opposite, is eternal? There is no time in bliss. All the clocks were thrown out of heaven."

Henderson enters Africa in desperation, leaving behind the wreckage of his relations with his wife, his children, and humanity in general, refusing to accept the fact that he must perish. He emerges from Africa having faced death knowingly and willingly, and bearing its living symbol (the lion cub containing the spirit of Dahfu) in his arms. He has ceased to become and begun to be.

Considered one by one, the adventures of Henderson are plausible, though improbable; taken as a whole they attain legendary dimensions and Henderson himself assumes the stature of a folk hero. His adventures, of course, are also a quest (since he wears a red wool hunting cap, readers of *The Catcher in the Rye* immediately identify him as a quester). Echoes of legends reverberate throughout the novel. For example, Henderson, returning to Danbury on the train, gets drunk and plays solitaire in the club car: "I was talking aloud and groaning and the cards kept falling to the floor," he says. In Danbury he then "lay on a bench in the station swearing, 'There is a curse on this land. There is something bad going on. Something is wrong. There is a curse on this land!'" The curse on the land, of course, is the curse of Eliot's modern wasteland, and Henderson's swearing is obviously not profanity: it may involve an unspoken, still unconscious vow. And the deck of cards, which "kept falling," vaguely suggests the Tarot deck of *The Wasteland*. The title of the novel and the connection of the Wariri with *From Ritual To Romance* makes it clear that the fertility quest is central.

Henderson, as everyone has noticed, is conspicuously removed from the urban Jewish world which Bellow evokes in all of his earlier novels. In fact, the removal is *too* conspicuous. The prose of *Henderson* echoes the rhythm and idiom of

Jewish speech. Henderson himself says, in a passing remark about a resort hotel, that it was "an elegant establishment, they accept no Jews, and then they get me, E. H. Henderson. The other kids stopped playing with our twins, while the wives avoided Lily." Henderson, in effect, is a super-Jew—a superman and a pariah not because of his race, but because of his extraordinary humanity. His life history is a satirical commentary on the ideal American of the D.A.R.; with social ties to the Adamses and Jameses, with three million in the bank, Henderson now can love only pigs, and his social role is the desecration of his family estate and his pedigreed heritage.

It is a wildly comic conception of the all-American hero, and Henderson's adventures are often hilarious. The ironies involved in the confrontations of the various cultures are endless. The main irony, perhaps, is that Henderson, who appears as savior to the primitive cultures, brings salvation only to himself. The Arnewi are rid of the frogs, but lose the water too; the Wariri are given rain, but robbed of their god-king. *Henderson* is full of these ironies; it is a looking-glass view of human history, at once totally insane and totally perceptive.

Like all of Bellow's novels it is a technical tour de force, a unique achievement. Unlike the others, however, it is acted out in regions entirely removed from the real world. Henderson's America is no more real than his Africa. The strangeness of his experience reflects the strangeness of the human condition, and the unreality of the novel is a commentary on the unreality of the "real." Critics who have complained of the unreality of Henderson's America have not seen through the looking glass.

But whether the looking-glass view of *Henderson* is more effective than the double vision of *The Victim* and *Seize the Day* is another question. Because of the huge conception and scope of *Henderson*, its effect is necessarily more diffuse. In *Henderson* the real world is only implied, shown only through the looking glass. This conception is more suggestive, more open-ended, than the double vision, but lacks its inherent strength, in which the real and imaginary worlds actively reinforce each other.

To the close reader of Bellow's earlier work, *Herzog* (1964) is not a particularly surprising book—certainly not in the sense that *Augie* must have been surprising to readers of *Dangling Man* and *The Victim*. *Herzog* is written in the freewheeling style which he unveiled in *Augie* and developed in *Henderson*. Philosophically too, *Herzog* represents an amplification of Bellow's earlier ideas rather than a radical new departure.

But if there is no great qualitative difference, there certainly is a quantitative one. Moses Elkanah Herzog is the first of Bellow's heroes to earn his living as an intellectual. One of his problems, in fact, is that his response to life is an intellectual rather than a more natural, instinctive one. His relations with everyone are glossed with a running psychological and philosophical commentary. His sexual relations with his mistress must be thoroughly analyzed; her bed is also the analyst's couch, and the two functions are concurrent. Even with his little daughter June, Herzog is always aware of the implications to her of his every word and gesture. He can't be natural.

Herzog had had all the credentials of the "promising" intellectual: a Ph.D., teaching positions at metropolitan universities, two respected books on the "history of ideas," and several grants from a large foundation. But like all of Bellow's heroes, he is now undergoing a crisis. His second marriage has ended in divorce, he has had to abandon his teaching, and he is driven by a compulsion to re-examine his whole philosophical position, which he thought had been safely "synthesized." His first wife Daisy has the custody of his son Marco, and his second wife Madeleine his daughter June. His brothers don't understand him; most of his friends have sided with the wives; and Valentine Gersbach, his closest friend, has become Madeleine's lover. Herzog's only real human relationship now is his affair with Ramona Donsell, a "priestess of Isis" who owns a flower shop in New York and is approaching forty. Driven to the edge of paranoia by his experience with Madeleine, Herzog suspects Ramona's motives.

His suspicions are understandable: Madeleine had made a fool of him. After persuading him to give up his position at a university to buy an old house in the Berkshires, she found she was bored with life in the country, and insisted that they move to Chicago so that she could do graduate work in Slavonic languages. Herzog had to find a new job not only for himself, but for Madeleine's lover as well—and even a private school for little Ephraim Gersbach. By submitting to Madeleine's every whim, Herzog only increased her loathing for him, until at last she ordered him to leave his own house and furnished his photograph to the police so that he could not disturb her *liaison* with Valentine.

Herzog is now contemplating the wreckage of his life. He pours out his grievances in countless letters—some real, most imagined—to his wives, his lovers, his psychiatrists (he has one in New York and one in Chicago), his friends, his colleagues, to politicians, philosophers, theologians, the New York *Times,* the Secretary of the Interior, the President, to the living and the dead, to God. Like all of Bellow's heroes, Herzog is hypersensitive. But he surpasses the earlier heroes in the scope and complexity of his response to life and in his determination to meet it head-on, without evasion, without "ideal constructions" of any kind. Herzog's world, which he had thought he understood, has collapsed. He is driven to question his first premises, to rethink his entire position. His synthesis has come unstuck.

Herzog's is the typical crisis of the contemporary intellectual. His relentless search for a viable world-view (*"What this country needs is a good five-cent synthesis,"* he notes) makes *Herzog* the richest of Bellow's works ideologically. In general, Herzog's attitudes are Bellow's own, and they are consistent with those of the earlier spokesmen—Joseph, Schlossberg, *et al.* Themes from the earlier work recur in *Herzog.* Man's need to believe in reason, his alienation in an irrational world, his need for a sense of community, the intensity of his life in the face of the ultimate fact of death— these themes had become prominent as early as *Dangling Man.* Readers of *The Victim* will recognize in *Herzog* such familiar themes as the deformation of character which results from our shutting others out of our lives, the meaning of "human," the acceptance of human finitude, the incomprehensible complexity of truth, and the significance of choice in determining the quality of life. The acceptance of the risks involved in exposing one's inmost being to others, the need to oppose the modern view of man as a specialized functionary rather than an intrinsically valuable person, the essential purity of man's desires, and the dilemma of the modern man who must make rational choices without enough facts—these themes from *Augie* are prominent in *Herzog* as well. The importance of the here-and-now is revealed to Herzog as it had been to Wilhelm in *Seize the Day*. Readers of *Henderson* will be prepared for several themes in *Herzog:* man's infinite "want" or longing in the face of his finitude, the power of the human mind, the difference between becoming and being, the exposure of the illusion of an "untroubled but eternal life," and the illusion of a "deal" with fate.

This is not to suggest, however, that *Herzog* is mainly a recapitulation of Bellow's earlier ideas. Some of the ideas prominent in the earlier books—e.g., the question of freedom of the will in *Dangling Man,* the problems of anti-Semitism and moral responsibility in *The Victim,* the search for a worth-while fate and the "leap" ("easy or not at all") in *Augie*—are not prominent in *Herzog*. Even though it is probably the most comprehensive single statement of Bellow's ideas, *Herzog* has a focus all its own, and in at least one respect it may represent a departure from his earlier thought.

Herzog's first academic studies had been concerned with the Romantic movement. He had begun with the political philosophies of the seventeenth century, "clear, hard theorems," and had moved toward the "mass convulsions" of our own time: "What he planned was a history which really took into account the revolutions and mass convulsions of the twentieth century, accepting, with de Tocqueville, the universal and durable development of the equality of conditions, the progress of democracy. . . . his study was supposed to have ended with a new angle on the modern condition, showing how life could be lived by renewing universal connections; overturning the last of the Romantic errors about the uniqueness of the Self; revising the old Western, Faustian ideology; investigating the social meaning of Nothingness.

And more." His studies led him to conclude, like many other contemporary thinkers, that man's environment is now so radically different from that of the Age of Reason that it has revolutionized "what it means to be a man. In a city. In a century. In transition. In a mass. Transformed by science. Under organized power. Subject to tremendous controls. In a condition caused by mechanization. After the late failure of radical hopes. In a society that was no community and devalued the person. Owing to the multiplied power of numbers which made the self negligible. Which spent military billions against foreign enemies but would not pay for order at home. Which permitted savagery and barbarism in its own great cities. At the same time, the pressure of human millions who have discovered what concerted efforts and thoughts can do."

Man seems to have a compulsive need to synthesize, to make coherent sense out of the apparent absurdity of his world, to feel that his life has some transcendent meaning. Herzog writes, *"People are dying—it is no metaphor—for lack of something real to carry home when day is done. See how willingly they accept the wildest nonsense."* Herzog himself, above all else, "thought and cared about belief. (Without which, human life is simply the raw material of technological transformation, of fashion, salesmanship, industry, politics, finance, experiment, automatism, et cetera, et cetera. The whole inventory of disgraces which one is glad to terminate in death.)" Much like Augie March, Herzog is confronted by beliefs, by evangelists of one sort or another, at every hand. Herzog's problem is Augie's—and Joseph's and Leventhal's and Wilhelm's and Henderson's—to maintain his identity and integrity and to find a solid ground for belief in the flood of advice and ready-made "systems" which people try to force upon him.

The focus of all these systems, of course, is their view of man. It is here that the fundamental assumption—the "leap," really—has to be made. And it is here that we find the fundamental paradox: "Suppose, after all, we are simply a kind of beast, peculiar to this mineral lump that runs around in orbit to the sun, then why such loftiness, such great standards?" On the level of simple experience, the paradox is perhaps even more striking. Herzog is haunted by his childhood, by the mystery of his mother's love, by the poignance of her gesture of moistening her handkerchief to wipe his face, a gesture which he remembers now, forty years later, as if it had happened a moment ago. To him the gesture is symbolic of man's dilemma: "All children have cheeks and all mothers spittle to wipe them tenderly. These things either matter or they do not matter. It depends upon the universe, what it is." To Herzog, as to all of Bellow's heroes, the gesture has meaning. He cannot believe otherwise.

Yet Herzog, a theorist himself, has come to distrust the systematic interpretations of human nature: *"Man has a nature, but what is it? Those who have confidently described it, Hobbes, Freud, et cetera, by telling us what we are "intrinsically," are not our greatest benefactors. . . . Modern science, least bothered with the definition of human nature, knowing only the activity of investigation, achieves its profoundest results through anonymity, recognizing only the brilliant functioning of intellect. Such truths as it finds may be nothing to live by, but perhaps a moratorium on definitions of human nature is now best."* In one of his letters he writes that *"the problem as I see it is not one of definition but of the total reconsideration of human qualities. Or perhaps even the discovery of qualities."*

The current systematic views of man offend Herzog's sense of man's transcendent importance, his intrinsic individuality and worth, his complexity. Man's life is too complicated, too mysterious, too real, too immensely significant (too holy, perhaps) to be reduced to a formula. Herzog writes:

we mustn't forget how quickly the visions of genius become the canned goods of the intellectuals. The canned sauerkraut of Spengler's "Prussian Socialism," the commonplaces of the Wasteland outlook, the cheap mental stimulants of Alienation, the cant and rant of pipsqueaks about Inauthenticity and Forlornness. I can't accept this foolish dreariness. We are talking about the whole life of mankind. The subject is too great, too deep for such weakness, cowardice. . . . A merely aesthetic critique of modern history! After the wars and mass killings! . . . As the dead go their way, you want to call to them, but they depart in a black cloud of faces, souls. They flow out in smoke from the extermination chimneys, and leave you in the clear light of historical success—the technical success of the West. Then you know with a crash of the blood that mankind is making it—making it in glory though deafened by the explosions of blood. Unified by the horrible wars, instructed in our brutal stupidity by revolutions, by engineered famines directed by 'ideologists' (heirs of Marx and Hegel and trained in the cunning of reason), perhaps we, modern humankind (can it be!), have done the nearly impossible, namely, learned something.

In another letter, to his Chicago psychiatrist, Herzog writes: *"I've read your stuff about the psychological realism of Calvin. I hope you don't mind my saying that it reveals a lousy, cringing, grudging conception of human nature. This is how I see your Protestant Freudianism."* These views of man—views by professional philosophers and theologians and historians and psychologists—are too far removed from the real thing, from "ordinary experience," to suit Herzog: *"Very tired of the modern form of historicism which sees in this civilization the defeat of the best hopes of Western religion and thought, what Heidegger calls the second Fall of Man into the quotidian or ordinary. No philosopher knows what the ordinary is, has not fallen into it deeply enough. The question of ordinary human experience is the principal question of these modern centuries, as Montaigne and Pascal, otherwise in disagreement, both clearly saw.—The strength of a man's virtue or spiritual capacity measured by his ordinary life.*

One way or another the no doubt mad idea entered my mind that my own actions had historic importance. . . ."

All of these theorists Herzog calls *"Reality instructors. They want to teach you—to punish you with—the lessons of the Real."* This view of life, Herzog thinks, "was becoming the up-to-date and almost conventional way of looking at any single life. In this view the body itself, with its two arms and vertical length, was compared to the Cross, on which you knew the agony of consciousness and separate being." But Herzog cannot accept the high value currently placed upon suffering: *"the advocacy and praise of suffering take us in the wrong direction and those of us who remain loyal to civilization must not go for it. . . . More commonly suffering breaks people, crushes them, and is simply unilluminating."*

In his disenchantment with suffering, Herzog seems to move away somewhat from Bellow's earlier heroes, who, if they did not advocate suffering, still found it spiritually therapeutic. Henderson, in fact, had called it "about the only reliable burster of the spirit's sleep." Leventhal's ordeal in the "depths of life" had given added dimension to his character. So had Joseph's, and Augie's, and Wilhelm's. And so, we must conclude, has Herzog's. His final acceptance of Ramona, in the aftermath of his crisis, is a more meaningful acceptance because of that crisis: it goes beyond acceptance, in fact, to commitment.

This commitment is not miraculous, however; it is inherent in Herzog's character. It is implied in his criticism of Dr. Edvig's "lousy, cringing, grudging view of human nature" and in Herzog's contempt for the *"Reality instructors."* His commitment, even in the depths of life, is always to nature and to life. Despite his hurt and his jealousy toward Madeleine and Valentine, he manages to be affirmative and magnanimous: "And if, even in that embrace of lust and treason, they had life and nature on their side, he would step quietly aside. Yes, he would bow out." His attitude toward little June is similar: "There was much to be seen in that house on Harper Avenue [Madeleine's love nest]. Let the child find life. The plainer the better, perhaps." Through all his troubles Herzog manages to retain his faith in what he calls the "inspired condition":

to live in an inspired condition, to know truth, to be free, to love another, to consummate existence, to abide with death in clarity of consciousness—without which, racing and conniving to evade death, the spirit holds its breath and hopes to be immortal because it does not live—is no longer a rarefied project. . . . the technology of destruction has also acquired a metaphysical character. The practical questions have become the ultimate questions as well.

Annihilation is no longer a metaphor. Good and Evil are real. The
inspired condition is therefore no visionary matter. It is not reserved
for gods, kings, poets, priests, shrines, but belongs to mankind and
to all of existence.

This essential, incorrigible faith and optimism, which all his
suffering can only temper, pulls Herzog through.

The tempering effect of suffering is important, and Herzog
is no pollyanna: his optimism ignores none of the "lessons of
the Real." But at times he had wished, quite naturally, to forget about the existential abyss, to ignore the depths of life,
to try to make a deal, like Henderson, with fate: "He wondered
a times whether he didn't belong to a class of people secretly
convinced they had an arrangement with fate; in return for
docility or ingenuous good will they were to be shielded from
the worst brutalities of life. . . . he considered whether he
really had inwardly decided years ago to set up a deal—a
psychic offer—meekness in exchange for preferential treatment." What the deal amounts to is an attempt to restrict the
dimensions of life in order to minimize the risk of exposure.
In minimizing our vulnerability to suffering, we also minimize
our possibilities for transcendence. As Herzog puts it, "I
thought I had entered into a secret understanding with life
to spare me the worst. A perfectly bourgeois idea. On the
side, I was just flirting a little with the transcendent."

Herzog cannot carry out his deal with fate because he cannot submit to the imprisonment of his soul. To do so would be
to deny the driving force of his being: his faith in the il-
limitable power and glory of the human spirit. The soul, he
feels, "lives in more elements than I will ever know." This is
the faith behind his refusal to accept, however much he would
like to, any of the precooked syntheses of the human condition: "human life is far subtler than any of its models," he
insists. The models may be intriguing, sophisticated. "But they
are constructions," not reality. Herzog, like Bellow's first hero
Joseph, is fascinated by "ideal constructions." But faced with
the choice between the theory and the reality, between
artificial light and living darkness, Herzog, like Joseph, must
choose the dark reality, humanity.

The "constructions" can account for everything in man except the unaccountable, the soul. Herzog says, "We have ground to hope that a Life is something more than such a cloud of particles, mere facticity. Go through what is comprehensible and you conclude that only the incomprehensible gives any light." The soul is incomprehensible: we don't know what it is, or how or why it operates, but we seem to be stuck with it: "Can't dump the sonofabitch, can we?" Herzog's friend Sissler remarks. "Terrible handicap, a soul." It lives in more elements than we will ever know. The man who exposes himself to these elements is, in a strictly practical sense, a fool. But he is, to quote old Schlossberg once again, fully human.

A man can choose, of course, to live an insulated life, to make a deal with fate, to ignore the existential abyss. But in doing so he loses his soul, for the transcendent meaning of the soul lies not only in its relation to the infinite, but also in its individuality: "Three thousand million human beings exist, each with *some* possessions, each a microcosmos, each infinitely precious, each with a peculiar treasure. There is a distant garden where curious objects grow, and there, in a lovely dusk of green, the heart of Moses E. Herzog hangs like a peach." One of the most seductive temptations of our time, Herzog recognizes, is the temptation to trade this individual microcosmos for a place in a system less "infinitely precious," perhaps, but more widely accepted and understood. But the man who has sold his soul for social success, the "non-fool . . . who bent the public to his will . . . the organizational realist," has paid a price unacceptable to Herzog.

In refusing to pay that price, Herzog has made a conscious, admirable, perhaps even heroic, choice. Although he is a failure, a fool, a ridiculous figure by popular standards, he has kept his microcosmos alive—not by shielding it from the elements, but by opening it to them. Insularity and conformity, in Herzog's lexicon, are synonymous with atrophy. Although his soul may live in more elements than he will ever know, he has grasped the essentials: the soul *lives*, and it lives *in the elements*.

Adrift in an indifferent world, burdened with a soul whose

longings he does not understand, Herzog still manages, like Conrad's Lord Jim, to commit himself to the elements and, by his struggling, somehow to remain afloat. This constant struggle—intellectual, spiritual, emotional (in fact, in more elements than we know)—against drowning seems to be inherent in the human condition. But the struggle, Herzog finally concludes, has a metaphysical dimension; it encompasses wonder as well as suffering.

Man's struggle, then, does not have to be given a systematic meaning. It is vaster, richer, more complex than any meaning man could assign to it. Reality instructors try to assign such a meaning because they cannot see the obvious, and they hope for immortality because they cannot, or fear to, live in the here-and-now. Their ambitious models of life are a caricature of the real thing, because the soul lives in more elements than we can hope to know. But the fact that it does live is all we need to know. We can then commit it freely to the elements, in full awareness of our folly and our mortality, but unafraid and with our transcendent vision unimpaired. As Herzog himself expresses it, "Hitch your agony to a star."

As the last few pages have illustrated, discussions of *Herzog* tend to become summaries of its ideas. This is almost inevitable because of the nature of the book itself—a vast compendium of observations and aphorisms on the human condition. Disjointed as they seem to be, they nevertheless, when taken as a whole, define a philosophy of life which is deep, comprehensive, and coherent. It is the fullest statement of Bellow's own view; and despite the irony and comedy inherent in the narrative conception, Herzog is closer than any of the other heroes to Bellow himself.

Although the story is told in the third person, the narration becomes so deeply involved in Herzog's consciousness that the effect is close to that of *Dangling Man:* the portrait of a man trapped in his own consciousness. The novel is saved from becoming static by the vivid scenes in which Herzog encounters the real world or remembers his encounters with it. Some of these are among the best that Bellow has done.

Nevertheless, they remain a series of vignettes, united mainly by their relevance to Herzog's emotional crisis.

The account of that crisis is framed between the first page and a half and the last chapter, where the resolution is explained and developed. The first sentence of the novel, "If I am out of my mind, it's all right with me, thought Moses Herzog," announces both the problem and its resolution. We learn in the third sentence that Herzog is now "confident, cheerful, clairvoyant, and strong"; and his expression at the end of the brief first section is "weirdly tranquil" and "radiant." The first sentence is a brilliant beginning; the matter-of-fact acceptance of insanity is a curious announcement, and we can't wait for an explanation. It is embedded in the next three hundred pages.

Surprisingly, it turns out to be rather simple: Herzog had loved Madeleine and lost her; but when she finally appeared in the Chicago police station, he saw her at last for the bitch she really was. Realizing that he is better off without her, Herzog is ready for the world again. It is, in fact, *too* simple. It is too unrelated to Herzog's monumental anguish. He is not a satirical folk hero like Henderson, even though the most meaningful dimension of his existence is in his own imagination. That imagination is the most impressive among Bellow's heroes, but it is the imagination of a man who, unlike Henderson, exists in the real world. Bellow never shows that Herzog's feeling for Madeleine is large enough to precipitate all this suffering. For example, the scene in which Madeleine tells Herzog they are through is very well handled, but it is satirical; and Herzog's feelings, so coldly analytical throughout the encounter, necessitate something other than the emotional crisis which the scene supposedly triggers. Although Herzog is said to dread "the depths of feeling that he would eventually have to face," we are never really shown these depths in terms of their stated determinant. As many critics have noticed, sexual relationships are seldom convincing in Bellow's fiction.

Although *Herzog* is not as perfectly realized or convincing as *The Victim* or *Seize the Day*, it is the most impressive of Bellow's novels in its intellectual and philosophical range. And even though Herzog's relationship with Madeleine is not fully developed enough to "cause" his crisis, his intellectual anguish itself is very real. In fact, *Herzog* comes close to being the definitive portrait of the problems and anxieties of contemporary intellectuals.

The evocation of the reality of intellectual anguish, never more powerful than in *Herzog*, is the major achievement of Bellow's work as a whole. Though his other heroes are not professional intellectuals, their crises are of intellectual and philosophical nature and origin. Bellow's fiction is the richest and deepest view of these problems in contemporary American literature. And his best work also has a psychic dimension which, though not explored as deeply or as fully as in the work of Norman Mailer, can be convincingly real. It is most real, in fact, when it is not explicit—as in the irrational acts of Joseph, or in the moving early chapters in *Augie*. Bellow's heroes are all initiated into what Leventhal called the "depth of life," and it is their discovery of this depth which enables them to discover their own humanity.

But the passionate intellectual concern of Bellow's fiction can also become a limitation. His most recent work has become increasingly pedagogic. It is often a view of ideas rather than of life, and human experience is used as a gloss on Bellow's theories about it. Fascinating as Herzog's observations are, what is their final relevance? Though Herzog's imprisonment in his own ideas is part of Bellow's message, the world outside the prison is not made convincing enough (e.g., in Herzog's sexual relationships). The heroes are always initiated into a larger reality which is implied rather than shown. A definition of this reality, of course, would be too much to ask. Not even Faulkner could define it. But Faulkner shows us more of the "elements," to use Herzog's term, in which the soul lives.

The intensity of Bellow's ultimate concern is magnified by his technique. Each of his novels is a brilliant and original conception; each creates its own unique view of the human condition, in which the form itself becomes meaning. In *Henderson* the created view is wholly imaginary, though it has an uncanny relevance to "reality." In the other novels the created views encompass both the real and imaginary worlds. The way in which the two worlds are made to reinforce and explain each other is Bellow's major technical achievement.

Human life, Bellow said in a recent lecture, is ultimately a mystery.[18] The exploration of this mystery, in all its complexity and contradiction, is the purpose of his art. Man in that art is a finite creature in a world of infinite complexity, in a sense the helpless victim of vast forces beyond his understanding or control. Yet in the most important sense, man himself is the measure of all things and is, therefore, what he chooses to be. In the bewildering world of the twentieth century, Bellow says, man may seem to be nothing. But he is obviously something. Exactly what he is, and therefore what he will become, is purely a matter of personal choice. For even though countless influences offer him an infinity of fates, each man is what he chooses to be. And because of the range of human possibilities, what he chooses to be can be great indeed.

This choice is an act of faith. But it is not the simple faith of Augie March, nor is it based (like many of the contemporary creeds which Herzog abhors) upon an oversimplified view of man and his heritage. Bellow's work, seemingly offhand and effortless, reveals beneath the surface a mind which is imaginative yet disciplined and which assumes that all of human thought is relevant to the present human condition. In Bellow's view, faith is not a reflex action; it must be earned through the consideration of the full range of human experience, and it cannot exist without knowledge of profound despair. In his lecture on recent American fiction, Bellow attacked the "unearned bitterness" of many modern novelists, a bitterness which they learned from writers of earlier generations rather than from life itself. As a reflex rather than an "earned" attitude, this bitterness lacks integrity.

18. Saul Bellow, *Recent American Fiction* (Washington: Library of Congress, 1963), p. 12.

Bellow's own integrity has assured the stature of his work; he is already a contemporary classic. He offers neither easy optimism nor unearned bitterness; and his honest, inspired, and relentless examination of the human condition has given his work an interest which is both timely and timeless.

three

J. D. SALINGER
– through the glasses darkly

Although Salinger was publishing stories as early as 1940, serious interest in his work was slight until *The Catcher in the Rye* (1951) occasioned a belated deluge of critical comment. In 1963 the "Salinger industry" (the term is George Steiner's) reached its high-water mark, with almost 40 percent of the volume of the Faulkner industry—big business indeed. But a reaction had already set in. In that year the first book-length study of Salinger turned out to be disappointing in its critical judgment and strangely hostile toward Salinger himself. Many other critics had begun to scold him for an increasing social irresponsibility, obfuscation, and obsession with Eastern philosophy and religion, and for the narrow exclusiveness of his view of life—in short, for his failure to develop in directions which the critics could approve of. These attacks were often spiced with personal animosity—of the kind usually associated with attacks upon, say, Norman Mailer—and the word used more and more to describe

Salinger's talent and achievement was "minor."

But the fact is, as James E. Miller, Jr., has maintained in his recent pamphlet,[1] that Salinger is not minor. Even if he were to stop writing now, which is not likely in spite of his much discussed "silence," he has produced a novel and a series of stories which are close to being perfectly realized works of art. They have unity, coherence, and depth; they are exceptionally well made in a way that Bellow's fiction (except for *The Victim* and *Seize the Day*) is not. And although Salinger has a rich comic sense, his vision is of the utmost seriousness and deserves to be taken seriously. It is a mark of this seriousness that Salinger is vulnerable to parody. He has not only a unique style, but also a single mindedness and an openness (despite the self-protective gestures of his characters) which almost invite parody, as well as ingenious readings and highly personal responses from his critics.

While these critics do not agree on the ultimate value or meaning of Salinger's achievement, they do agree that a pattern of development exists. His early stories for the slick magazines are interesting only in a rather limited technical and historical sense (Salinger himself has tried to suppress them). The stories which he has thought worth preserving have all been published since 1947. "Franny" (1955) marks the beginning of his preoccupation with the Glass saga, his major work. But the best place to begin is with *The Catcher*.

The Catcher in the Rye is a story of initiation. Its hero, Holden Caulfield, is innocent but not altogether naive; he has some knowledge of evil though he is not himself corrupted by it. His story is an odyssey—a search and a series of escapes, both a flight and a quest. The odyssey itself, which begins on a Saturday afternoon "last Christmastime" at Pencey Prep and ends at the New York zoo on Monday afternoon, is placed in a retrospective frame; Holden tells the story some months later in California, where he has been seeing a psychiatrist.

1. James E. Miller, Jr., *J. D. Salinger* ("University of Minnesota Pamphlets on American Writers," No. 51 [Minneapolis: University of Minnesota Press, 1965]).

The central conflict in *The Catcher* is the traditional one between innocence and experience. Holden has a messianic sense: he wants to save people from sin—their own and the world's. But like most messiahs, he fails: he learns that it is impossible to be the catcher in the rye, to save the innocents from the fall into experience. As the frame of the book suggests, the story itself is both a case study and a therapeutic confession.

As we would expect of a piece of therapeutic confession literature, *The Catcher* is filled with Holden's aversions. The most obvious aversion is to phoniness. Everyone in the book, except for Holden's little sister Phoebe, is a phony, pretending to be someone he is not. At Pencey Prep, for example, the phonies include the students themselves, Mr. Spencer whose Mr. Chips pose is a travesty of a teacher's ideal concern for his students, the undertaker-trustee who is so grotesque that Holden feels that the only adequate comment on him is the one made by a student during the trustee's speech in chapel— a "terrific fart." Holden has the most sympathy for the phonies who are obviously flawed, whose poses are defensive. Ackley, for example, is physically repulsive, Sunny the prostitute is stupid, Mr. Spencer is insecure.

Holden responds to these people with kindness and generosity, but when they try to touch him physically or emotionally, he must withdraw. His response to Mr. Antolini, his former English teacher and a surrogate father to him, is typical. When he is safely out of Antolini's apartment and his fear and revulsion have passed, he says "I wondered if just maybe I was wrong about thinking he was making a flitty pass at me. I wondered if maybe he just liked to pat guys on the head when they're asleep." The incident is left ambiguous.

Because Antolini had fallen from the pedestal on which Holden had placed him, the boy over-reacted. This pattern, typical of adolescent relationships, is shown also in Holden's relationship with Sally Hayes and implied in his feelings about his older brother D. B. and his father. Holden recognizes the power of the forces which oppose innocence and integrity, and is fighting a delaying action against them. Waiting for Phoebe at the museum, he thinks that Phoebe will see the same exhibits that he himself saw years before: "Certain things they should stay the way they are. You ought to be able to stick them in one of those big glass cases and just leave them alone." But in the scene in which Holden descends into the tomb, he finds under the glass case the familiar obscenity, which leads to his climactic realization that "You can't ever find a place that's nice and peaceful, because there isn't any. You may *think* there is, but once you get there, when you're not looking, somebody'll sneak up and write 'Fuck you' right under your nose. Try it sometime. I think, even, if I ever die, and they stick me in a cemetery, and I have a tombstone and all, it'll say 'Holden Caulfield' on it, and then what year I was born and what year I died, and then right under that it'll say 'Fuck you.' I'm positive, in fact." Holden learns here that the conflict is inevitable, inescapable, eternal. And later, watching Phoebe and the other children on the carrousel, he realizes that "if they want to grab for the gold ring, you have to let them do it, and not say anything. If they fall off, they fall off, but it's bad if you say anything to them." Innocence is transitory, but all the more beautiful and poignant for being so. This is the truth which has Holden "damn near bawling" as Phoebe goes round and round and the carrousel plays "Smoke Gets in Your Eyes."

It was inevitable that *The Catcher in the Rye* would be compared to that greatest American odyssey of initiation, *Huckleberry Finn*. The most striking similarities between the books are in their narrative framework, their episodic structure, their colloquial style, and their social criticism.

Huck Finn introduces himself in the first paragraph as the narrator of his story, and in the last paragraph he remarks that "there ain't nothing more to write about, and I am rotten glad of it, because if I'd a knowed what a trouble it was to make a book I wouldn't a tackled it and ain't agoing to no more." These two paragraphs mark the limits of Huck's consciousness of his audience and of his own role as narrator—unless we interpret occasional phrases like "you see" as indications of that awareness. Salinger uses a similar frame for *The Catcher:* Holden introduces himself in the first paragraph, and returns to an explicit concern with his narrative role in the last three. But his consciousness of that role, unlike Huck's, does not become entirely submerged in the main part of the story. It is evident in the self-consciousness of his speech, "if you want to know the truth." Throughout the book Holden remains keenly aware of his audience; his "you," unlike Huck's, is specific.

This self-consciousness reduces the opportunity for dramatic irony somewhat, but does not destroy it. Though Holden is not as naive as Huck, he is not as sophisticated as Salinger or, hopefully, Salinger's audience. He is not sophisticated enough to be aware of the archetypal nature of his odyssey or its initiatory situations. And he does not learn as much from his experiences as the reader does. D. B. had asked him what he thought about his story; Holden tells us that "if you want to know the truth, I don't *know* what I think about it." But Salinger has given us enough information to know what to think about it. Dramatic irony, then, is not just possible; it is used effectively throughout the novel.

Holden's self-consciousness is not a flaw in the book, as some critics have maintained, but a primary source of its extraordinary power and interest. It is Holden's awareness of himself which makes his experience painful to him in a way that Huck's never is. The very inadequacy of his adolescent language becomes moving because it represents still another kind of irony—the tragic gulf between the magnitude of human suffering and the poverty of our means for understanding or even expressing it. Holden's awareness creates a powerful tension in his character and in the novel as a whole; he is conscious of being trapped in the no-man's-land between two worlds, between his beautiful but impossible ideals and a sordid but inescapable reality.

The language of *The Catcher in the Rye* is the instrument through which this tragic consciousness is conveyed. Salinger's ear for colloquial speech is perfect; he is in the same league with Mark Twain and Ring Lardner and Thomas Wolfe. And his control of the language in *The Catcher*, though never obtrusive, is unfailing. It is the instrument which, more than any other, gives the novel its overwhelming sense of real life.

Finally, the meanings of the odysseys of Huck and Holden seem to be much the same. The narrative frame in both books functions not only to give perspective and credibility to the story itself, but also to end the odyssey with a qualified acceptance of society. *The Catcher* ends with Holden's cryptic advice: "Don't ever tell anybody anything. If you do, you start missing everybody." This has usually been interpreted as a statement of Holden's reconciliation with society. Because "everybody" includes even "that goddam Maurice," the pimp who beat him up, Holden obviously is talking about forgiveness. But Holden's acceptance, like Huck's, is muted; it includes, rather than reverses, his philosophical and emotional estrangement from society. Like Huck, he knows what it is to be "sivilized"; he has "been there before."

Because the situation of Holden parallels so closely the known facts of Salinger's own adolescence, the question arises whether the novel may not be, in a sense, a *Künstlerroman* as well as a *Bildungsroman*, whether Holden may not be initiated into the vocation of art as well as the state of maturity. There is evidence within the story, as well as in Holden's "writing" of it, that this may be true. He has a reputation among his classmates as a writer, he has a critical interest in D. B.'s writing and in the movies and drama, and Mr. Antolini has apparently recognized his literary talents and interests. The last two sentences of *The Catcher*, then, may refer to Holden's vocation as well as to his qualified acceptance of society. As Joyce had shown in *A Portrait of the Artist as a Young Man*, one who enters the priesthood of art never fully enters society again. Although he ministers to society, he also passes judgment upon it and uses it as his raw material; he is always to some extent an outsider. "Don't ever tell anybody anything. If you do, you start missing everybody." You miss them because they are irrevocably lost, except in memory. Holden's acceptance of society is an acceptance of the fact that he will always be deeply estranged from its dominant social values and, in a sense, a stranger to its people as well.

Nine Stories (1953) collects all of Salinger's stories which he then thought worth preserving. They had been published over a period of exactly five years—from January 31, 1948 ("A Perfect Day for Bananafish") to January 31, 1953 ("Teddy"). All but two had appeared originally in the *New Yorker*. They are exceptionally well made, with the exquisite sense for telling details and the perfect ear for spoken language which readers of *The Catcher in the Rye* had come to expect. Their themes are similar to those of the novel; the stories show people trapped between transitory ideals and oppressive realities. The collection begins and ends with stories about suicide. The final story, however, reverses the view of the first; Teddy's death, unlike Seymour's, is a transcendent, triumphant act.

Like Salinger's earlier stories, these have a quality of melodramatic slickness. This tends to obscure their depth and seriousness, which become more pronounced toward the end of the five-year period. Each story presents a climactic epiphany, or revelation. In some of the stories this epiphany is essentially despairing, a revelation of the isolation, frustration, and corruption inherent in man's fate. But in other stories the epiphany is ultimately hopeful, a revelation of the real human values which can live even in the presence of theoretical despair. Significantly, this hope seems to grow somewhat stronger in the later stories, several of which foreshadow the desperate hope of the Glass saga itself.

The first story is a document in that saga. "A Perfect Day for Bananafish" is an especially shocking story because the reader is completely unprepared for Seymour's suicide, coming as it does at the end of a comic story which reaches its climax in the hilarious incident in the elevator. Salinger himself viewed the story as an inadequate "explanation" of Seymour's suicide; later in the Glass saga he has Buddy admit authorship of the Bananafish story and discuss its limitations. Since it is an integral part of the Glass legend, we shall return to it later.

The second story, "Uncle Wiggily in Connecticut," has been explored extensively by critics. Although their close readings have revealed the very deliberate craftsmanship and the closely woven texture of the story, "Uncle Wiggily in Connecticut" is really a rather simple but compelling vignette. Eloise Wengler, a suburban housewife, gets drunk in the afternoon with her former schoolmate and comes to a realization that her own unhappiness is destroying her daughter. Denied entry to the magical world of the Glasses (her boyfriend Walt Glass was killed in an accident in Japan), Eloise has married a boring phony, and she takes revenge upon him, her daughter, and her colored maid, Grace. Eloise's final words, "I was a nice girl, wasn't I?" are a recognition of her corruption, a despairing cry for help that her shallow, vicious girlfriend Mary Jane would not answer even if she understood it.

But in "Just Before the War with the Eskimos," an inarticulate cry for help is answered. Ginnie, fifteen, goes home with her girlfriend Selena to collect some money which Selena owes her for cab fare. There she meets Selena's brother Franklin, a physical and psychological mess, rejected both by the army and by Ginnie's older sister, to whom he had written eight unanswered letters. After a long conversation which reveals Franklin's despair, Eric, an older man who had worked with Franklin in a war plant, arrives to take him to the movies. Ginnie realizes that Eric is a homosexual; and when Selena finally returns with the money, Ginnie tells her to forget it and suggests that they get together that night. A few questions that she "casually" asks Selena about her brother show the nature of her concern: evidently she is trying to save Selena, or Franklin, or both. Psychologically, they are orphans, with a father who loves his job and a mother who loves her hypochondria. Although Ginnie's reaching out to them is a perfect example of what Ihab Hassan has called "the rare quixotic gesture" in Salinger, it seems doomed to failure. The gesture itself is all that keeps the story from despair.

In "The Laughing Man" the narrator looks back to 1928, when he was nine, to tell about the Comanche Club, a glorified babysitting operation run by John Gedsudski, a law student at NYU. After school and on Saturdays and holidays, John rounds up the Comanches and takes them in his old bus somewhere sufficiently far from their parents. John, a short and rather ugly young man, is "extremely shy, gentle. . . . an Eagle Scout, an almost-All-American tackle of 1926. . . , loved and respected"—worshipped, in fact—by the Comanches. When he needs to kill time with them or to get them settled down in the bus after a hard game of ball, he spins out another installment of a fantastic, fascinating, and seemingly interminable story about a grotesque hero called the Laughing Man, who masks his hideous face with poppy petals. The legend of the Laughing Man reflects John's own private fortunes, and perhaps his inner view of himself as well; it becomes even more inventive and expansive after the entry of Mary Hudson, a former Wellesley girl, into John's life. Although the boys resent her at first, they accept her because she is fun and because she makes the "Chief" happy. But one day the relationship between the Chief and Mary seems strained; she finally runs off crying. In the bus John takes up his story again; but apparently reflecting his own feelings, he has the Laughing Man smash his life-sustaining vial of eagles' blood, pull off his mask, and die—all because of the death by treachery of his beloved timber wolf. The Comanches are badly shaken: the youngest bursts into tears; and the narrator, after seeing a scrap of tissue paper (which reminds him of the poppy-petal mask) flapping uselessly against a lamppost, arrives home with his "teeth chattering uncontrollably and was told to go right straight to bed." When John pulls the mask off the Laughing Man he also unmasks himself; and the young narrator, only vaguely aware of the reasons for the unmasking, can only feel its pain. The laughter behind the mask of poppy petals turns out to be the dark laughter of the knowledge of evil entering into the world of innocence, a world which can never be the same again.

"Down at the Dinghy," like "Uncle Wiggily in Connecticut," is a peripheral Glass story. Boo-Boo Tannenbaum (nee Glass) discovers that her son Lionel has run away again. She finds him sitting in the family dinghy and learns that he is upset because he overheard the maid call his father "a big—sloppy—kike." Lionel thinks she meant "kite." Boo-boo brings him back with promises of pickles and a boat ride with Daddy. But the reconciliation here, as in *The Catcher*, is a desperate one: Boo-Boo, shaken by the maid's remark, realizes the pervasive entrenchment of anti-Semitism and knows that she cannot shield her son from it forever.

"For Esme—with Love and Squalor," probably Salinger's best-known short story, is also one of his most optimistic. Much of its interest and effectiveness is derived from the narrative framework itself. The anonymous narrator, we learn in the first paragraph, has been invited to a wedding in England set for April 18, 1950. Because it is impractical for him to go, he has "jotted down a few notes on the bride as I knew her almost six years ago." His notes, he says, are intended not to please, but "to edify, to instruct." He then tells how he met the bride on his last afternoon in Devonshire in April, 1944. After packing his gear he had wandered into town, where he had watched a children's choir practice, and after leaving the church, had gone to a tearoom. There Esme, one of the choir girls, had exchanged guarded smiles with him and had then come to his table to talk. He is fascinated by her character, an incogruous blend of innocence and maturity, and by her personality, at once nervous and poised, shy and vivacious. Because of her habit of getting straight to the point, they learn a great deal about each other in their brief conversation. Her father, a nobleman, had been killed in North Africa, and she protects her six-year-old brother Charles from this tragic fact by spelling the word "slain" for the narrator. Their mother is dead also, and the children live with an aunt. Esme learns that the narrator is married, and she promises to write to him first so that he won't feel "compromised." The remark illustrates Esme's attempt, which the narrator finds very moving, to understand the adult world into which her experiences have forced her far too early (she is only about thirteen) and too "extremely" (significantly, her favorite word). When she learns that he is an aspiring writer, she has him promise to write a story for her which will be "extremely squalid and moving."

The next pages are the story which the narrator had promised her. It concerns a Sergeant X. As the narrator and Esme had parted, she had said that "I hope you return from the war with all your faculties intact." But when we next see him as Sergeant X, he is far from intact: his fingers tremble, his face twitches, he aches all over, he is (like so many of Salinger's protagonists) nauseated, and he must press his temples to keep his brain in place. He has been in an army hospital with a nervous breakdown. Now he sits at his desk in a house in Gaufurt, Bavaria, and tries to pull himself together. He keeps returning to a copy of Goebbels' *Die Zeit Ohne Beispiel* in which the spinster daughter of the displaced German family had written "Dear God, life is hell." Then X annotates the woman's despair with a quotation from Dostoevski: "Fathers and teachers, I ponder 'What is hell?' I maintain that it is the suffering of being unable to love."

The woman's note and the words of Dostoevski explain the reason for X's breakdown: the inability to love. Sergeant X, the German spinster, and indeed all of humanity have been swept into the unprecedented era of which Goebbels wrote. X's salvation appears in the form of a package from Esme which contains a note and her father's wristwatch. Her message opens a window once more in X's soul: "Then, suddenly, almost ecstatically, he felt sleepy." The darkness of despair has been dispelled by love, and communication between X and the world has been re-established.[2]

The story is designed "to edify, to instruct" us in the belief that love and innocence, so incongruous and even apparently ridiculous in a world ravaged by hatred and depravity, can

2. This denouement echoes that of an earlier Salinger story, "A Boy in France," *Saturday Evening Post*, CCXVII (March 31, 1945), 21, 92, in which a soldier in France, exhausted by combat and shocked by finding small pieces of a dead German in his foxhole, reads a letter from his younger sister and then is able to fall asleep. The soldier is Babe Gladwaller, the friend of Vincent Caulfield. In another early story, "Last Day of the Last Furlough," *Saturday Evening Post*, CCXVII (July 15, 1944), 26–27, 61–62, 64, Sergeant Gladwaller, like Sergeant X, reads Dostoevski's Father Zossima.

still redeem that world in moments of radiance. This desperate hope is presented more subtly and more convincingly, perhaps, in Salinger's later work, but never with more impact than in "For Esme—with Love and Squalor."

In "Pretty Mouth and Green My Eyes," a lawyer's lovemaking is interrupted by a phone call from a younger colleague who is worried about an erring wife and a collapsing career. As the story develops, it becomes increasingly apparent that the girl in the lawyer's bed is the colleague's wife. Skillfully made and psychologically accurate, the story achieves considerable impact. The colleague's contemptibility is gradually revealed as the real reason for his wife's faithlessness. And the older lawyer, using his colleague's suffering to enhance the wife's admiration for his own maturity and stability, is no less contemptible. This story is perhaps the darkest view of modern life in the collection.

Salinger's next story, "De Daumier-Smith's Blue Period," is a milestone in his career. Salinger himself apparently considered this story significant; he selected it for inclusion in *Nine Stories*, even though it had not been published originally in a prominent magazine, as the other stories in that collection had.[3]

Jean de Daumier-Smith is the pseudonym used by the narrator of the story during his career as an instructor at Les Amis Des Vieux Maîtres, a correspondence art school in Montreal operated by Monsieur I. Yoshoto and his wife. The nineteen-year-old Daumier-Smith's relations with the inscrutable Yoshotos and then with his students are grotesque enough to remind us of Nathaniel West. Daumier-Smith is, in fact, a sort of Miss Lonelyhearts to those who wish to escape from the dreary prison of their everyday lives through art: his first two students are Bambi Kramer, a young Toronto housewife whose idols are Rembrandt and Walt Disney; and R. Howard Ridgefield, a fifty-six-year-old Windsor "society photographer" who submits a picture showing "the familiar,

3. The story originally appeared in the London *World Review* (May 1952). Why the *New Yorker* rejected it is a mystery; it is much better than some of Salinger's earlier publications in that magazine.

everyday tragedy of a chaste young girl, with below-shoulder-length blond hair and udder-size breasts, being criminally assaulted in church, in the very shadow of the altar, by her minister."

Daumier-Smith's third student, Sister Irma of the Sisters of St. Joseph, has real talent. A teacher in a convent elementary school near Toronto, she is innocent, naive, almost illiterate, and fiercely determined to learn all she can about drawing, so that she can teach it to her "kittys." Her best picture is a water color, on brown paper, of the procession to the sepulchre in the garden of Joseph of Arimathea.

Daumier-Smith stays up past four in the morning working with Sister Irma's lesson and writes her a long, impassioned letter which she apparently shows to her superiors; in the return mail M. Yoshoto receives a letter saying that Sister Irma will no longer be able to study at the school. Daumier-Smith writes another letter to her, which he never mails, and less than a week later Les Amis Des Vieux Maîtres is closed down for operating without a license.

In his brief career at the school Daumier-Smith experiences two revelations, both of which involve the display in the window of the orthopedic appliances shop on the ground floor of the building which also houses the correspondence school. Both revelations are essentially religious. The first occurs the night before the school receives the letter disenrolling Sister Irma. Looking into the window of the shop Daumier-Smith is struck with the realization that "no matter how coolly or sensibly or gracefully I might one day learn to live my life, I would always at best be a visitor in a garden of enamel urinals and bedpans, with a sightless, wooden dummy-deity standing by in a marked-down rupture truss."

This thought is an almost unendurable revelation of despair: Daumier-Smith cannot hope to be a possessor of truth; he will always be a gawking and uncomprehending spectator, lost in a world in which a "sightless, wooden dummy-deity" neither sees the suffering of man nor acts to assuage it. When Daumier-Smith calls himself "a visitor in a garden" he is obviously thinking of Sister Irma's painting of the garden of

Joseph of Arimathea, with the broken body of Christ being followed by a few mourners and a crowd of spectators. For Duamier-Smith, "the major figure in the picture was a woman in the left foreground, *facing* the viewer. With her right hand raised overhead, she was frantically signalling to someone— her child, perhaps, or her husband, or possibly the viewer—to drop everything and hurry over." Sister Irma's painting, despite all its flaws in technique, had confronted Daumier-Smith with a new insight: that the essential meaning of human existence is religious and understood by only a few, although the events in which it is hidden are viewed by multitudes. Because of its ability to communicate a genuine insight, this painting by a naive, ignorant Sister of St. Joseph is truly a work of art, while the slick, sophisticated work of Daumier-Smith himself is nothing more than competent craftsmanship. If Sister Irma and Daumier-Smith were to appear in Joseph's garden, she could be one of the women of Galilee, but he could be only one of the crowd. So shocking is this insight that Daumier-Smith does not really assimilate it until four days after he has first seen the painting of the garden.

In an attempt to escape from the terror with which his revelation has filled him, Daumier-Smith thinks of his pupil. He imagines her as shy, beautiful, innocent, and eighteen. He imagines that she has not taken her final vows, that he rescues her from the convent, and that they walk away together "toward a far, verdant part of the convent grounds, where suddenly, and without sin, I would put my arm around her waist. The image was too ecstatic to hold in place, and, finally, I let go, and fell asleep." The similarity to "Esme" here, of course, is striking: in both stories the protagonist has been terrified by the existential void and calmed by the vision of a young girl's innocence so that he is able to fall asleep.

The next evening, brooding over Sister Irma's disenrollment, Daumier-Smith experiences his second revelation. Returning to the school at twilight, he sees "a hefty girl of about thirty" changing the truss of the wooden dummy in the shop window. The girl is startled to find him watching her, steps back onto a stack of irrigation basins, and falls heavily. Flushed and embarrassed, she rises and resumes lacing the new truss. According to Daumier-Smith, "It was just then that I had my Experience. Suddenly . . . the sun came up and sped toward the bridge of my nose at the rate of ninety-three million miles a second. Blinded and very frightened— I had to put my hand on the glass to keep my balance. The thing lasted for no more than a few seconds. When I got my sight back, the girl had gone from the window, leaving behind her a shimmering field of exquisite, twice-blessed, enamel flowers." Later that evening, Daumier-Smith writes in his diary "I am giving Sister Irma her freedom to follow her own destiny. Everybody is a nun."

The revelation that everybody is a nun is essentially the same revelation of a later story, "Franny": everybody is Seymour's Fat Lady (*i.e.*, Jesus Christ). The insight given to Daumier-Smith is that we are all imperfect, and that each of us must serve in his own way. The heavy, self-conscious, clumsy woman of thirty in the shop window is human; but Daumier-Smith's beautiful, trusting, graceful Sister of eighteen has been an idealization, and worse, a delusion.

The figure of the dummy-deity becomes less puzzling after the second revelation. The dummy's sightlessness and woodenness do not bother Daumier-Smith this time; in fact, he scarcely notices the dummy at all in his preoccupation with the woman and the enamel flowers. The scene in which the woman laces up the truss on the dummy-deity may imply that God exists primarily as a model created by men, for men, and that we serve God only to serve men.

The enamel basins and bedpans and urinals which Daumier-Smith formerly associated with pain and suffering he now sees as flowers. Although they are associated with suffering, their purpose is to ameliorate it. They are "twice-blessed," perhaps because mercy "blesseth him that gives and him that takes," or perhaps blessed once by the service performed by the woman in the shop window and again by the light of revelation. In the service of others, Salinger seems to be saying, we ourselves become sanctified, or at least purified; and in the blinding light of truth even the plainest instruments of service must glisten. Sister Irma, therefore, must be freed to follow her own destiny.

"Teddy" is the last of the *Nine Stories* and Salinger's last story before the real beginning of the Glass saga with "Franny." "Teddy" marks the first appearance of Salinger's interest in Eastern religions. Like "Daumier-Smith," "Teddy" is filled with grotesque characters: Teddy McArdle, the ten-year-old seer; his fatuous, whining father whose beautiful voice is familiar to listeners to several of the most popular radio serials; his embittered mother; his vicious little sister Booper; and Bob Nicholson, an education student who is rude, hypersensitive, cynical, overbearing, and not very bright. Teddy is first seen in his parents' stateroom on an ocean liner returning from Europe. They send him to find Booper. After telling her to go to the stateroom, he sits in a deck chair and looks through his diary. He is joined before long by Bob Nicholson, who somewhat cynically draws him into a philosophical discussion. In pointing out to Nicholson that it is ridiculous to fear death, Teddy mentions that when he and Booper go to the ship's pool for their swimming lesson, they might find it drained for cleaning and his sister might push him in and he might die of a fractured skull. Nicholson, on an impulse, decides to go to the pool after Teddy has left for his lesson. He has not quite reached the pool when he hears a little girl scream.

Teddy's death, which he had foretold so calmly and accurately, thus puts the stamp of authenticity on his matter-of-fact claims to mystical insight, and we are forced to regard him not as a psychotic child but as a genuine seer. Teddy's indifference to his own death is a corollary of his belief in Vedantic reincarnation, which he discusses as naturally as someone else might mention the weather. "All you do," he says, "is get the heck out of your body when you die." It is the state of the soul, not the body, which must concern us.

"Life is a gift horse in my opinion," Teddy writes in his diary.[4] What counts is "spiritual advancement," which can continue from one incarnation to the next.

"I was six when I saw that everything was God," Teddy says, and "I could get out of the finite dimensions fairly often when I was four." Teddy's spiritual advancement is so far along that he feels that through concentration he could bring into his conscious mind the knowledge of how to grow his own body. And Teddy's psychic insight extends into the future as well as the past. Since he can predict the future, Teddy has a special insight into human destiny. Since the future is "latent" in the present, in the sense that certain present events will make certain future events more likely to occur, and since Teddy can see into the future, it would seem that he could literally control his own fate.

Teddy can and does control his fate, but not in the superficial sense. He does not rush to buy a thousand shares of Amalgamated X because he knows it will rise twenty points in the next week; he does not even attempt to avoid his swimming lesson. Although he could do these things, he knows that they have nothing to do with spiritual advancement. He is more interested in achieving a mystical comprehension of the unity of being, in merging his soul with the great soul of God. Teddy is contrasting this ultimate concern with the shabbiness of most human desires when he says that "most people don't want to see things the way they are. They don't even want to stop getting born and dying all the time. They just want new bodies all the time, instead of stopping and staying with God, where it's really nice."

Teddy says that it is hard to meditate and to lead a spiritual life in America, and the final half dozen pages of the story are an attack on the type of mind which relies on "logic and

4. Salinger's seers are inveterate diarists. Seymour keeps one, as did Daumier-Smith. Teddy, with extraordinary powers of both recall and prescience, uses his diary primarily to remind himself of mundane details which he might otherwise forget, although he does record an insight here and there, as if to guide his meditation when he reviews the diary.

intellectual stuff." The direction in which we must turn for true knowledge is inward.

If this point of view were confined to "Teddy," the story could be read almost as the reduction to absurdity of Zen as a guiding principle of human conduct. Yet Salinger's seriousness is verified by later work, especially "Zooey" and "Seymour." One critic, Tom Davis, has maintained that "Zen is, in fact, the dominating force in most of his later fiction." [5] It is the emergence of this interest in Zen, together with the growing distrust of reason, which makes "Teddy" an important story in Salinger's development. It is an excellent finale for *Nine Stories* because it provides a bridge between the predominantly social concerns of Salinger's earlier work and the essentially religious concerns of the Glass stories.

The first of the Glass stories is "A Perfect Day for Bananafish" (1948). But the five major documents in the saga thus far are "Franny" (1955), "Raise High the Roof Beam, Carpenters" (1955), "Zooey" (1957), "Seymour: An Introduction" (1959), and "Hapworth 16, 1924" (1965). "Franny" and "Zooey" are concerned with Franny's nervous breakdown, and the other three with Seymour. Buddy Glass, two years younger than Seymour, is the narrator of all the stories but "Franny," which is told in the third person by an unidentified narrator who could possibly be Buddy also. As Buddy tells us in the most recent installment, "for a good many years of my life— very possibly, all forty-six—I have felt myself installed, elaborately wired, and, occasionally, plugged in, for the purpose of shedding some light on the short, reticulate life and times of my late, oldest brother, Seymour Glass, who died, committed suicide, opted to discontinue living, back in 1948, when

---

5. Tom Davis, "J. D. Salinger: 'The Sound of One Hand Clapping,' " *Wisconsin Studies in Contemporary Literature*, IV, i (Winter 1963), 41–47. In this interesting article, Davis concludes that the influence of Zen has been, on the whole, harmful to Salinger's art. Especially relevant is his citation of Arthur Koestler's comment, in *The Lotus and the Robot*, that Zen is "a kind of moral nerve-gas" which blurs the distinctions between good and evil which are socially necessary. Davis identifies *unity* and *detachment* as the Zen principles which appeal to Salinger. Both principles are prominent, of course, in Teddy's philosophy.

he was thirty-one." In the process of shedding light Buddy has ranged through more than forty years of family history, quoting letters and diaries, reconstructing conversations, and providing his own commentary on the prodigious Glasses. The complexity and subtlety of Salinger's narrative technique, in fact, may itself be the major achievement of the saga.

"Franny" is the account of the inauspicious beginning of a weekend which Franny is spending with Lane Coutell, her boyfriend, at an unnamed Ivy League college. Lane meets her at the train and takes her to lunch, where she tries to tell him about the deep despair which she is experiencing. But Lane doesn't listen; he is too busy illustrating, unintentionally, just what Franny is talking about: the tawdry egotism of the academic world. Franny, after giving way to her feelings in the ladies room, returns to the table and, pressed now by Lane for an explanation of her strange behavior, tries to communicate once again. But when he tells her he loves her, she feels faint again, and finally comes to in the manager's office, mumbling her Jesus prayer: "Lord Jesus Christ, have mercy on me."

"Zooey" is the story of Franny's recovery. She is now at home in the Glass apartment, lying on the living room couch. Her brother Zooey is in the bathtub reading a four-year-old letter from Buddy. Their mother Bessie enters the bathroom twice for long discussions about Franny. Zooey then goes to the living room, but unable to lift Franny out of her depression, goes to the room of Seymour and Buddy, from which he calls Franny on Seymour's private telephone. After hearing Zooey's revelation that Seymour's Fat Lady is really "Christ Himself," Franny is overcome by joy and falls into a "deep, dreamless sleep."

"Raise High" is Buddy's view of Seymour's wedding to Muriel in 1942. Seymour does not show up, and Buddy leaves in a cab with a couple and a little old man who turn out to be the matron of honor, her husband, and Muriel's great-uncle. After the cab is stalled in a parade, Buddy takes the wedding guests to the apartment which he and Seymour had shared. A phone call later reveals that Seymour has eloped with

Muriel. In the bathroom Buddy reads Seymour's diary—a useful antidote to the poisonous view of Seymour expressed by the matron of honor.

"Seymour" is Buddy's deepest and most anguished attempt to "explain" his brother. It is, as Professor Miller has pointed out, "not so much a story as an assemblage of notes, observations, anecdotes, and irrelevancies . . . , much like Buddy's (or Salinger's) journal, from which a story might one day be made. . . . [It has] the form that conceals form, with all the seemingly irrelevancies deliberately designed to create an even greater than usual illusion of reality." [6] The story tells us more, perhaps, about Buddy than about Seymour. It reflects an emotional crisis in Buddy's own life, and his return to the world at the end parallels Franny's return at the end of "Zooey."

"Hapworth," published in the New Yorker, June 19, 1965, is the most recent installment of the Glass saga. In this long (28,000 words, by Time's count) story, Buddy's role is confined to writing a four-paragraph introduction and "typing up an exact copy of a letter of Seymour's that, until four hours ago, I had never read before in my life." The letter was written to the family from a camp in Hapworth, Maine, where Seymour and Buddy, aged seven and five, were spending the summer. Its structure is similar to that of "Seymour: An Introduction." The letter ranges from Seymour's analysis of himself, Buddy, the campers, and the counselors (including Mrs. Happy, in whom he has a precocious sexual interest), to advice to his parents and his younger brothers and sister, to philosophy and religion (God is already a source of wonder and joy to Seymour), to prophecy. It closes with a long list of books (with copious asides on the follies of reformers and scholars, and further paeans to God and Christ), and a final prophecy concerning Buddy's literary achievements. It includes some tantalizing bits for the Glass biographers (e.g., that Les had grown up in Australia) and, in the manner of

6. Miller, *J. D. Salinger*, p. 42.

"Teddy," a number of offhand references to "previous appearances." [7]

As the introduction to "Hapworth" acknowledges, the character of Seymour is Buddy's central obsession. We first meet Seymour, in "A Perfect Day for Bananafish" (1948), during the last hour of his life. As the title suggests, the parable of the bananafish is at the heart of the story. Seymour tells the story to a little girl, significantly called Sybil, whom he meets on the beach:

"This is a *perfect* day for bananafish."

"I don't see any," Sybil said.

"That's understandable. Their habits are very peculiar. *Very* peculiar." He kept pushing the float. The water was not quite up to his chest. "They lead a very tragic life," he said. "You know what they do, Sybil?"

She shook her head.

"Well, they swim into a hole where there's a lot of bananas. They're very ordinary-looking fish when they swim *in*. But once they get in, they behave like pigs. Why, I've known some bananafish to swim into a banana hole and eat as many as seventy-eight bananas." He edged the float and its passenger a foot closer to the horizon. "Naturally, after that they're so fat they can't get out of the hole again. Can't fit through the door."

"Not too far out," Sybil said. "What happens to them?"

"What happens to who?"

"The bananafish."

"Oh, you mean after they eat so many bananas they can't get out of the banana hole?"

"Yes," said Sybil.

"Well, I hate to tell you, Sybil. They die."

"Why?" asked Sybil.

"Well, they get banana fever. It's a terrible disease."

---

7. Seymour's most specific revelation is that in his previous appearance he corresponded with Sir William Rowan Hamilton. Like Seymour, Hamilton (1805–1865) was a boy wonder; at the age of seventeen he discovered an error in Laplace's *Mécanique céleste,* and went on to a brilliant career in mathematics. He was also like Salinger in one respect: the last sentence of the entry on Hamilton in the *Encylopaedia Brittanica* tells us that "Hamilton was a neat, precise and fastidious writer; this may be the reason that he published so little compared with the extent of his investigations."

The parable of the bananafish is apparently an allegory of Seymour's own spirit. His banana fever, which seems to be a form of spiritual gluttony, is not very well defined by the rest of the story, even in Muriel's telephone conversation with her mother, which shows Seymour from his wife's point of view. As a result, his suicide has been given a wide variety of critical interpretations. The passage already quoted, however, is fairly explicit. Bananafish are born, not made, and Seymour's extreme sensitivity is inherent, not developed; he was born with it just as he was born with the tendency to have thin hair. Bananfish "lead a very tragic life," Seymour says. Why tragic? Can a creature which merely follows its natural instincts be considered tragic? Seymour may mean that the bananafish is destroyed by the very qualities which differentiate it from other fish, just as the classical tragic hero can be destroyed by the swelling up of some essentially good aspect of his character to such proportions that it distorts that character and dislocates his position in the natural order of things. Seymour's sensitivity, the very aspect of his character which enables him intuitively to understand and love other people, has grown cancerous. It has led him to live on a level of intensity which these other people cannot share and which he himself cannot sustain. Even little Sybil, to whom Seymour tells the parable of the bananafish, is essentially selfish and insensitive; the subtlety of the story eludes her, as well as the meaning of his remarks about Sharon Lipschutz. Sybil is interested mainly in being entertained; when Seymour cuts short her ride and pushes the float toward the shore she says goodbye and "ran without regret in the direction of the hotel."

Then, ascending in the elevator to his room and his death, Seymour makes one final, fleeting, unsatisfactory attempt to communicate with humanity. He notices a woman staring at his feet. But when he mentions this to her, she denies it and turns away:

"'I *beg* your pardon. I happened to be looking at the floor,' said the woman, and faced the doors of the car.

'If you want to look at my feet, say so,' said the young man. 'But don't be a God-damned sneak about it.'

'Let me out of here, please,' the woman said quickly to the girl operating the car.

The car doors opened and the woman got out without looking back."

Like Sybil, the woman in the elevator does not look back. She is thinking only of herself, and she sees Seymour's remarks not as a revelation, or a communication, or even as a cry for help, but simply as an affront, an intrusion on her privacy, and a breach of etiquette. But her response is socially normal, typical of the response to Seymour by Muriel and the world: intellectual incomprehension and indifference, and emotional resentment.

As William Wiegand has pointed out, "In general, the bananafish diagnosis applies to all the Salinger invalids." [8] But Wiegand's description of the bananafish syndrome (the invalid "has no capacity to purge his sensations. He is blown up like a balloon, or like a bananafish, with his memories") is not entirely accurate. Holden Caulfield, for example is quiet capable of purging his sensations—e.g., in his quarrels with everyone.

Seymour's syndrome is characterized instead by a lack of emotional inhibitions, together with extreme sensitivity. It is only within their own family that the Glasses can find an environment which is not hostile to this freedom and sensitivity. Franny, for instance, would have understood Seymour's parable of the bananafish. But Seymour himself is trapped in a world which does not understand, where even his own wife is a "spiritual tramp" aware only of her own selfish needs. It is a world where bananas are the only food, and they kill him with their mushy blandness.

In "Seymour" we learn that he has always been a bundle of raw nerve ends: "I'm too keyed up to be with people. I feel as though I'm about to be born. Sacred, sacred day. The connection was so bad, and I couldn't talk at all during most of

8. William Wiegand, "Seventy-Eight Bananas," in Henry A. Grunwald (ed.), *Salinger: A Critical and Personal Portrait* (New York: Pocket Books, 1963), p. 137. Originally published as "J. D. Salinger: Seventy-Eight Bananas," *Chicago Review*, XI (Winter 1958), 3–19.

the call. How terrible it is when you say I love you and the person at the other end shouts back 'What?'" This passage, from Seymour's diary just before his wedding, illustrates the dilemma which he ultimately solves, or perhaps only avoids, by taking his own life. He is always too keyed up for outsiders, and his communications with them are always frustrated by a bad connection.

"Hapworth," however, now opens the possibility that Seymour's suicide was a positive act, a transcendent declaration of faith, just as Teddy's death had been. "Hapworth" reveals that Seymour had known that he would live "a generous matter of thirty (30) years or more," and that a gray-haired Buddy would survive to write about him. Perhaps his "monumental work to be done in this appearance, of partially undisclosed nature" is mainly the inspiring of Buddy. At any rate, the endowment of Seymour with all of this fantastic mystical insight has reopened the possibilities of interpretation of Seymour's character. Presumably, Buddy is now pondering these possibilities.

Buddy himself obviously suffers from Seymour's syndrome—in the form in which we saw it up until the revelations of "Hapworth." Buddy feels the need to communicate with the outside world, but is unable to do so effectively. In his introduction to "Zooey" he had shown an awareness that some critics do not get, or perhaps do not appreciate, his message. In "Seymour: An Introduction" this awareness has become an obsession. But Buddy is not easily discouraged. He sees himself as a disciple of Seymour, and even though he confesses his "perpetual lust to share top billing with him" in "Seymour," thus far he has still acknowledged him as master. He even pays to keep Seymour's private phone in the family apartment, perhaps as a kind of "hot line" to the hereafter.[9] Yet Buddy is not just a disciple, but an evangelist, organizing Seymour's insights and proclaiming them to the world.

Zooey, a television actor, is about ten years younger than Buddy, who was born, like Salinger, in 1919. It is he who manages to pull Franny back from the brink of a nervous

9. This is the phone which Zooey uses to give Franny the saving message that Seymour's Fat Lady is everyone—and Jesus Christ.

collapse. He resents both Buddy and Seymour for making "freaks" of the younger Glasses: he confesses to Bessie that he can't even sit down to a meal without repeating the Four Great Vows [10] which Seymour had taught him. "We're the Tattooed Lady," he tells Franny, "and we're never going to have a minute's peace, the rest of our lives, till everybody else is tattooed too." He attributes their alienation from society to the quiz-kids radio program, "It's a Wise Child," in which the Glass children performed, as well as to Seymour's mysticism. The Glasses, he feels, do not live their lives; they act them out.

Franny, five years younger than Zooey, is the baby of the family. Despite her prominence in "Franny" and "Zooey," she remains a rather shadowy figure, acted upon rather than acting. Like Holden Caulfield, she has an overwhelming sense of the phoniness of social institutions, and of the people those institutions produce—e.g., her date for the football weekend, Lane Coutell, is just such a caricature. But the saving message from Zooey about Seymour's Fat Lady restores Franny's faith and, like Sergeant X, she falls asleep.

The message which the Fat Lady symbolizes seems to be a mixture of Eastern and Western religious thought. It is Seymour, of course, who introduces the Glasses to Zen, and it appeals to them for several reasons. It is intuitive rather than rational, and the Glasses approach life intuitively. It deals with life directly rather than through the formulations of some metaphysical system, and the Glasses distrust theories. And it is introspective, teaching that the answers to the ultimate questions must be sought within each man himself; introspection appeals to the Glasses' sense of their own independence and importance. Obviously, Zen had been attractive to Salinger himself for some time; the epigraph to *Nine Stories* (1953) is a Zen koan:

We know the sound of two hands clapping.
But what is the sound of one hand clapping?

10. "However innumerable beings are, I vow to save them; however inexhaustible the passions are, I vow to extinguish them; however immeasurable the Dharmas are, I vow to master them; however incomparable the Buddha-truth is, I vow to attain it."

But in "Seymour" Buddy denies being a "Zen Buddhist, much less a Zen adept," and goes on to define his religious affiliations—or lack of them:

(Would it be out of order for me to say that both Seymour's and my roots in Eastern philosophy—if I may hesitantly call them "roots"—were, are, planted in the New and Old Testaments, Advaita Vedanta, and classical Taoism? I tend to regard myself, if at all by anything as sweet as an Eastern name, as a fourth-class Karma Yogin, with perhaps a little Jnana Yoga thrown in to spice up the pot. I'm profoundly attracted to classical Zen literature, I have the gall to lecture on it and the literature of Mahayana Buddhism one night a week at college, but my life itself couldn't very conceivably be less Zenful than it is, and what little I've been able to apprehend—I pick that verb with care—of the Zen experience has been a by-result of following my own rather natural path of extreme Zenlessness. Largely because Seymour himself literally begged me to do so, and I never knew him to be wrong in these matters.)

Buddy's philosophical point of view in the Glass saga thus far is fairly clear. At the heart of life is a great mystery which, as Zen maintains, can be apprehended only partially and intuitively. This mystery endows our individual lives with holiness (or spiritual mystery) as well: "Seymour once said that all we do our whole lives is go from one little piece of Holy Ground to the next. Is he never wrong?" Buddy says.

It is our individual lives which count; the outside world (or as Zooey puts it, "the joys of television, *Life* magazine every Wednesday, and European travel, and the H-Bomb, and Presidential elections, and the front page of the *Times,* and the responsibilities of the Westport and Oyster Bay Parent-Teacher Association, and God knows what else that's gloriously normal") is too complex and too far gone. If there is such a thing as a general social destiny, it is far out of our hands.

Social institutions are dehumanizing; organized society makes cowards and robots and phonies of us all. We really live only when we are in real communication with others. The most gifted among us, however, are also the most tragic since they have the greatest need to communicate (because they have the most ideas), but the greatest difficulty in doing so (because of the limitations of their audience).

The answer for these gifted people is humility, which alone can unite them with humanity. This is the answer which Zooey gives to Franny in the famous parable of Seymour's Fat Lady. It is the answer which Seymour thinks he sees in marriage: "above all, serve. . . . The joy of responsibility for the first time in my life." And it is the answer with which Buddy fortifies himself before going forth to face the twenty-four young ladies in "that awful Room 307. There isn't one girl in there, including the Terrible Miss Zabel, who is not as much my sister as Boo Boo or Franny. They may shine with the misinformation of the ages, but they shine."

Such climactic revelations of the need for love and the power of love were standard endings for Salinger stories even when he was writing for the slicks. In the Glass stories, however, these revelations have taken on an increasingly religious cast—so much so that it now seems that the ultimate significance of the series will be religious. From the bananafish story of 1948, which seemed to be entirely secular, Salinger has moved to "Hapworth," in which Seymour devotes page after page to talk about God.

Salinger's religious concern can be seen in the earlier stories, of course, and in *The Catcher in the Rye,* with its themes of the fall, the search for a father, and the descent into hell—even, perhaps, in its names (Allie) and symbols (Phoebe's blue coat). But *The Catcher* is evocative; "Hapworth" is explicit, a sermon. In one passage, for example, Seymour exhorts his family to

take your hats off to God, quite mentally, for the magnificent complications of the human body. Should it be so difficult to offer a brief, affectionate salute to this unfathomable artist? Is it not highly tempting to take off one's hat to someone who is both free to move in mysterious ways as well as in perfectly unmysterious ways? Oh, my God, this is some God we have! . . . to rely on God utterly, we must fall back on embarrassing, sensible devices of our own; however, they are not our own, which is another humorous, wondrous side of the matter; the embarrassing, sensible devices are His, too!

In a sense, these words are not Salinger's own. They are spoken by a seven-year-old genius who is convinced that he has extraordinary psychic insights and is trying to purge the "fustian" in his literary style. Yet after all the masks and ironies are stripped away, the religious position in this passage is the one toward which the Glass saga seems to be moving: the revelaton that whatever is, is right; that everything— even evil—is all a part of God's mysterious plan. Or as Seymour says earlier in "Hapworth," "one cannot even light a casual cigarette unless the artistic permission of the universe is freely given!"

This is not a revolutionary view; its most eloquent advocate was John Milton. But in Milton its corollary is a loud insistence upon man's freedom to make moral choices. The Glass saga, so far, has been moving away from these choices. Seymour made one in 1948 (at least, it seemed so at the time), and Franny rejected the world on moral grounds. Franny's reconciliation with the world was a moral choice too, an affirmation of her responsibilities as a member of the human race. But it was based upon revelation, the knowledge that Seymour's Fat Lady is Christ Himself, just as Buddy's decision to face the girls in 307 was based upon the revelation that all we do is move from one piece of holy ground to the next. Salinger's recent protagonists do not try to reform a corrupt world as Milton did, but find instead that its corruption is, in the blinding light of religious revelation, irrelevant.

As the focus of the saga moves inward, its outward action declines. The first story contains the most terrible act—Seymour's suicide; the most recent contains no direct action at all, but a recording of action described by Seymour and transcribed by Buddy. Salinger's fiction has grown increasingly reflective, concerned with internal action, with the filtering and analysis of external experience by the human consciousness.

The central consciousness which selects and analyzes the material is, of course, Buddy's. It is likely, therefore, that the real subject matter of the Glass saga is not Seymour, but the developing consciousness of Buddy. And our ultimate interest in Salinger, as in Henry James or Proust, may lie not so much in the externals which are recorded as in the central consciousness created to record them.

Critics of Salinger should remember that this central consciousness is a creation, that it is not necessarily identical with the consciousness of the author, even though it is part of it. In creating Buddy's awareness Salinger, like every other writer, has had to use his own experience and his own ideas. But it is a mistake to think that Salinger himself is not larger than Buddy, whose view is purposely limited.

Buddy's understanding of the Glass saga will always be incomplete. The important fact, however, is the development of that understanding. This is shown most dramatically in his changing attitudes toward Seymour. "A Perfect Day for Bananafish" recreates Seymour's suicide with the perspective which Buddy had in 1948. How much of the story is "factual" we do not know, and perhaps will never know; it is conceivable, though unlikely, that Buddy could have got most of the facts from the "witnesses," as he did with "Zooey." But the most important witness is his own. In the bananafish story we see a Seymour who is conscious of his own superiority, yet who expects as much of others as he does of himself. But in the later stories a different Seymour emerges each time, until in "Hapworth" we have Buddy discovering a Seymour who was, at seven, conscious of being unstable, but also of being "gloriously normal." Buddy's developing insight is a brilliant narrative device; it functions, like the multiple narrators in Faulkner's fiction, to suggest the multiplicity and elusiveness of final truth.

The increasing inwardness of Salinger's fiction, however, is also a limitation. Faulkner's characters, though imprisoned by their own limited views of reality, are always actively involved in the outside world; their imprisonment, in fact, is revealed in their interactions with that world. In the bananafish story and in "Franny" those interactions are shown, much as they were in *The Catcher in the Rye*, but the recent installments have been focused ever more sharply on the family itself; we are told about the outside world by Buddy, who quotes Seymour or one of the others. Although we see the Glasses in contact with the world in some of the stories, it is not the complex world which most of us know. It is, instead, Lane Coutell or Seymour's matron of honor. Salinger's skillful use of concrete details creates a certain reality in the Glass stories, but it is a surface reality. Beneath it is an essentially misanthropic view of life, in which the Glasses hold a monopoly on goodness, sensitivity, intelligence, and so on. The Glasses are a world in themselves, and in their world, so far, there has been little room for the complex adult relationships (sex,[11] for instance) which have traditionally been so prominent in the great family chronicles in fiction.

But the Glass chronicle is far from over, and Salinger has already shown that the interpretation of the earlier installments can be changed radically by later ones. It is already clear, also, that the stories are a significant technical achievement. The narrative conception is ingenious, and the Glasses themselves are interesting characters. And the ultimate meaning and relevance of their story can be judged only when all of the evidence is in.

The final stature of Salinger himself is still an open question, despite the current fashion of writing him off. *The Catcher in the Rye* is a major achievement, not only as a technical tour de force, but as a serious, relevant, and permanently interest-

11. Throughout Salinger's work, the closest relationships are between older brother and younger sister, mother and son, or brothers. These are relationships with strong sexual taboos. Even in "Pretty Mouth and Green My Eyes," in which sex is acknowledged (but not depicted), it is corrupting and destructive.

Salinger sometimes seems to use sexual vitality as a pejorative character trait. In "Zooey," for example, the names he assigns to the academicians (whom the Glasses regard with contempt) are interesting: Professors Tupper, Fallon, and Manlius, and Dean Sheeter. The last name "usually transports Franny when I mention it," Zooey says.

The fear of sex which the Glass brothers seem to share may have something to do with Bessie. They are all very conscious of her sexuality. Seymour compares her figure with Mrs. Happy's in "Hapworth," and throughout the bathroom scene in "Zooey" Buddy describes Bessie's crossing and uncrossing of her shapely legs. But when she admires Zooey's back and moves to touch it, " 'Don't, willya,' Zooey said, quite sharply, recoiling."

ing view of life: a classic. In the fifteen years since its appearance Salinger's published work has declined in quantity and developed in ways which seem far removed from that achievement. But from the beginning he has been a dedicated writer with confidence in his own talents, and the extraordinary success of his first novel gave him the independence he needed to pursue his vision. While that vision is obviously not yet clear to his readers, Salinger has had the conviction to follow it. In doing so he has produced fiction which is still puzzling in many ways, but far more interesting than a repetition of *The Catcher* or a return to the slicks would have been. Because of his sensitivity to criticism and his antipathy for critics, his relationship with them has become something of a cat-and-mouse game, the roles interchanging with each installment of the Glass saga.[12] But fortunately the main initiative in the game is still with Salinger.

12. The J. D. Salinger Special Number of *Modern Fiction Studies* XII, 3 (Autumn 1966) appeared too late for use in the present study, but should be mentioned because it contains several valuable critical articles and a very useful bibliography.

four

NORMAN MAILER
– a revolution in the consciousness of our time

The Naked and the Dead (1948) brought Norman Mailer unexpected and unnerving acclaim. But he turned his back on this easy success and began a deeper exploration of the contemporary consciousness than the technique of his first novel would allow. He has been savagely attacked for the "failure" of his later work, as well as for his unorthodox public opinions and behavior. It was over a decade after the publication of the first novel before critics, led by Norman Podhoretz,[1] began to realize that Mailer's own instincts were surer than those of his reviewers.

Structurally, *The Naked and the Dead* is well made; in an interview Mailer said that it was "written mechanically. . . . the work of a young engineer."[2]

1. Norman Podhoretz, "Norman Mailer: The Embattled Vision," *Partisan Review*, XXVI (1959), 371–91.
2. Steve Marcus, "Norman Mailer: An Interview," *Paris Review*, No. 31 (Winter-Spring 1964), 38.

Part One, "Wave," is a brief prologue which introduces the men of the reconnaissance platoon and takes them from the eve of the invasion to the first death on the beach. Part Two, "Argil and Mold," continues the differentiation of the human molecules of the wave and begins to develop the conflicts among the men as the nominal rank structure of the army is converted to a real power structure defined by the characters involved. The mold is superficially General Cummings, but really the war itself (Cummings is revealed in the "time machine" as a victim too); the soldiers, of course, are the clay. Part Three, "Plant and Phantom," is the climactic story of the reconnaissance patrol. Quoting Nietzsche, Mailer says that even the wisest among us "is only a disharmony and hybrid of plant and phantom." In the climactic patrol he shows how this fragmented nature operates. Part Four, "Wake," is a very brief epilogue which returns the situation to stasis: Cummings reviews the campaign, the surviving soldiers mop up the island and kill their prisoners, Major Dalleson returns to his first love, paperwork. The army is ready for the next stepping stone on the road to Tokyo.

Much of Mailer's technique is derived from Dos Passos.[3] The novel is panoramic in purpose, structure, and effect. The army, of course, is a ready-made microcosm which contributes much to the impact of *The Naked and the Dead*. Mailer uses "chorus" sections ("The Chow Line," "Women," "What Is a Million Dollar Wound?" "Rotation," "On What We Do When We Get Out") to stress the significance of his microcosm for any reader who might have missed it. And "time machine" sections are used to "explain" ten of the major characters as products of their environments. The cross section is carefully selected. Martinez, a Mexican, dreams of revenging himself upon white Protestant women. Goldstein is the suffering Jew. Wilson, a red-neck, illustrates the moral hypocrisy of the white-trash Southerner. Polack has been shaped by the slums,

3. In the *Paris Review* interview Mailer defines his literary idols as ". . . Farrell to begin with. Dos Passos, Steinbeck (I am trying to do it chronologically), Hemingway, and later Fitzgerald—much, much later. And Thomas Wolfe, of course," p. 43.

the Church, and the rackets; Brown by the crassness, shallowness, and dishonesty of the business world; Gallagher by the
"drabness, desolation, and waste" of the South Boston milieu.
Croft, the platoon sergeant, is a vicious Texan whose wife has
repaid his whoring in kind. Of the enlisted men in the platoon,
only Red Valsen has not been crushed by his environment;
although his deprivation has been severe, his sensitivity and
insight have made him the "wisest" of the soldiers.

The other two characters chosen for the "time machine,"
General Cummings and Lieutenant Hearn, objectify the polar
philosophical and political positions in the novel. Cummings is
a reactionary, a fascist, and Hearn is a disillusioned liberal.
Both are the sons of dominant, wealthy, boorish fathers whom
they rebel against. Cummings is sent to a military school and
to West Point; his father, concerned about the boy's interest
in sewing, painting, and music, hopes to make a man of him.
Hearn goes to a country day school and, like Mailer himself,
to Harvard.

Cummings is a latent homosexual; early in his marriage his
wife discovers "that he is alone, that he fights out battles with
himself upon her body," and she responds by seeking other
men. Cummings had given way to his homosexual impulses
only once, in Rome, but had been rolled by the man he picked
up, and has decided that the "thing that happened in the
Rome alley is a danger sign. . . . It must never come out
again." Although Mailer gives Hearn no overt homosexual
feelings or experiences, much of Hearn's "time machine" section (called "The Addled Womb") could be read in that way.
His mother typifies "the midwestern woman's denial of juice,"
and his father is a backslapping Babbitt who finds the juice
elsewhere. With a long series of women Hearn, like Cummings, finds himself alone. "You get me so goddam mad," one
of them tells him, "a million miles away, aren't you, nothing
ever hits you. Nothing's worth touching." Hearn's fascination
with the personal magnetism of Cummings could also be read
as an indication of Hearn's latent homosexuality, although
Mailer himself does not seem to intend that interpretation.

These two psychological case histories are shown to be the

basis of two polar philosophies. Cummings believes ardently in the primacy of the human will and in the survival of the fittest. He sees the army as an instrument for the exercise of personal power; Hearn sees him as a "nerve end with no other desire than to find something to act upon." Cummings believes that man is in transition from savage to god, that man's primary drive is to achieve omnipotence, that "the only morality of the future is a power morality, and a man who cannot find his adjustment to it is doomed. There's one thing about power. It can flow only from the top down." His obsession with power dates from the First World War, when he had watched an Allied attack upon the German lines and had been overwhelmed by an almost religious vision: "To command all that. He is choked with the intensity of his emotion, the rage, the exaltation, the undefined and mighty hunger." But after the Anopopei campaign, the general has to fight to hold onto his vision: "For a moment he almost admitted that he had had very little to do with this victory, or indeed any victory—it had been accomplished by a random play of vulgar good luck larded into a casual net of factors too large, too vague, for him to comprehend."

Although Hearn acknowledges the intellectual power and the personal magnetism of Cummings, he rejects his theories as simplistic and subhuman. Hearn's own dilemma is that of the modern liberal and humanist: he is unable to commit himself to simple solutions for incomprehensibly complex problems. His life has been a series of disillusionments—with parents, with prep school, with medicine, with radicalism, with literary criticism, with his jobs as a literary editor, union organizer, and radio copywriter, and with one woman after another. When Hearn discovers, in the last few days of his life, that he enjoys leading men, his reaction is typical: he is appalled to think that he may be no better than General Cummings or Sergeant Croft. But his decision to resign his commission is never carried out. He is killed in an ambush which the platoon blunders into because Croft had kept from him the real results of Martinez' scouting mission the night before. Hearn had tentatively decided to end the patrol after

an ambush the day before, but had been reluctant to face
Cummings "with empty hands, excuses, and failure." Hearn's
indecision and lack of faith in his own judgment, which by
now are habitual responses to every complex situation, are
partly responsible for his death.

If Mailer chose Cummings and Hearn to represent the clash
between the Fascist and liberal philosophies, he selected Red
Valsen to articulate the viewpoint of the common soldier. A
wanderer since the age of eighteen, Red has constantly fought
to maintain his identity in a world which seeks to rob him of
it. Although his wanderings have led him toward fatalism, he
has not accepted it. He knows that the long-range chances for
survival are slim, but he responds in a very practical way:
"There was nothing to do but to go from one day into the
next." Red has no illusions left. To an editorial sent by a relative to one of the men, which asked rhetorically whether the
GI's are dying in vain, Red answers "Of course they died in
vain, any GI knew the score. . . . fighting a war to fix something works about as good as going to a whorehouse to get
rid of the clap." Justice is irrelevant, both to the American
"cause" and to the destinies of the men themselves. Red,
drunk on jungle juice, tells his buddies, "You're all good guys,
but you're gonna get . . . the shitty end of the stick."

The other GI's, though they lack Red's insight, sympathy,
and integrity, are also aware of the abyss which may swallow
them at any moment. Although they try not to think about it, it
is never very far from their consciousness, and they have little
faith in the rituals which they invoke against it. Roth sneers
that "God is a luxury I don't give myself," and Goldstein, the
more pious of the two Jews, admits that "When the time
comes . . . they won't ask you what kind of Jew you are."
Even Ridges, the Southern fundamentalist, "had no hope; he
prayed to show that he was respectful."

The events of the novel, reinforced by Mailer's ironic commentary, illustrate a deterministic view of the war. General
Cummings' abilities in complex organization and planning are
shown to be almost irrelevant to the outcome of the campaign.

The climactic breakthrough occurs when he is away from the island, soliciting naval support which turns out to be unnecessary. Major Dalleson moves a platoon forward to occupy an abandoned Japanese bivouac and, in his confused and hesitant efforts to consolidate this new position, orders an attack which destroys, quite by accident, the hidden headquarters of the Japanese general. And the patrol, in which Hearn, Wilson, and Roth lose their lives, is conceived as a brilliant tactical maneuver by Cummings, but is really useless. In the report which Cummings submits to headquarters, the invasion of Botoi Bay which the patrol was intended to support is described as the decisive stroke of the campaign. Actually, the breakthrough directed by the fumbling Dalleson smashes the Japanese resistance, which was already weakened far beyond Cummings' knowledge by attrition and the naval blockade.

Thus the war is shown to be irrational, a series of almost random accidents, despite the huge, intricate military organizations which nominally direct it. It is, in the structural metaphor of *The Naked and the Dead,* like a wave whipped up somewhere far offshore, gathering amplitude and direction, crashing upon a beach, receding once again. Mailer's soldiers —even his general—are like the molecules of water involved; for them the process is random, the result of countless collisions with other molecules. The only fact is death, and confronted by that fact, man is naked. The wave itself is the campaign, the war, history; it has a certain pattern, but its origins, its ultimate end, and its significance are unknown.

Yet Mailer insists on searching for significance. His insistence is evident throughout the book: in the structure, the selection of characters and events, the "chorus," the "time machine," the constant philosophizing. Despite the high degree of verisimilitude which Mailer achieves in presenting the speech and actions of his characters, they remain puppets too obviously manipulated by the strategist and "engineer" of the great war novel. Like *U.S.A., The Naked and the Dead* is a thesis novel, and its treatment of the thesis is its major weakness. On the one hand, Mailer shows that his characters, especially those from the lower social classes, are conditioned by their environments. On the other hand, he sometimes shows that they help to create their own fates. There is no reason, of course, why Mailer should not deal with this paradox, which is a central one in all of literature. The weakness lies not in his failure to provide an answer to it, but in the shallowness of his exploration of the problem. And the weakness is an almost inevitable result of the structure of the novel, the attempt to "explain" so many characters. Like *U.S.A.* with its capsule biographies and its dozen easily forgettable major characters, *The Naked and the Dead* is a sociological tract.

And like *U.S.A.*, *The Naked and the Dead* is a very effective novel of social protest. Its characters illustrate the negative social results of bigotry and cultural deprivation. The army is not the only dehumanizing force in the book; there is a strong undercurrent of anger at the social attitudes which transform human values into mob values. And there is much in *The Naked and the Dead* to substantiate Dos Passos' view of America as poisoned by the Big Money, for which the antidote was a return to the principles of Jeffersonian democracy. Dos Passos had taken, in *One Man's Initiation—1918* and in *Three Soldiers* as well as in *U.S.A.*, a searching look at Wilson's war to make the world safe for democracy. But Mailer sometimes suggests deeper psychic reasons for the phenomenon of war. In the light of current discussions of the psychological aspects of war (the Eichmann case, the schizophrenic attitudes involved in the cold war, etc.), these reasons now seem more interesting than Dos Passos' indictment of the capitalists, however valid and relevant that argument may remain today.

In the characters of Cummings, Hearn, and Croft, and to a lesser extent with the other soldiers, Mailer touches upon the response to war as the fulfillment of certain basic psychic drives and needs. Norman Podhoretz has called Cummings and Croft the "natural heroes" of the book, and Mailer himself admitted that "Beneath the ideology in *The Naked and the Dead* was an obsession with violence. The characters for whom I had the most secret admiration, like Croft, were violent people." [4] Consciously, Mailer is contemptuous of Cummings and Croft—especially of Cummings' homosexuality—and of the irrationality of their attempts to prove their manhood through violence. But beneath this conscious contempt is the unconscious fascination, even admiration, which Mailer later realized and admitted, and which he has explored in his later work. Lieutenant Hearn is perhaps the most interesting of these case studies because Mailer created him at two distinctly different levels: on the surface his story is that of the disillusioned rationalist, a product of the countless defeats suffered by the liberals in the late 1930's; but at a deeper level, of which Mailer himself seems only partly aware, Hearn is dominated by a Calvinistic superego which shapes his responses to life in a pattern similar in many respects to the obsessions of Cummings and Croft, his theoretical opposites.

This concern with the psychic roots of social problems becomes central in Mailer's second novel, *Barbary Shore* (1951), which he has called "the first of the existentialist novels in America." *Barbary Shore* is indeed closer to Dostoevski than to Dos Passos; in it Mailer tried to capture "the air of our time, authority and nihilism stalking one another in the orgiastic hollow of this century." [5]

The narrator of *Barbary Shore*, Michael Lovett, is an unpublished novelist whose memory does not extend beyond the postwar period, presumably because of a war injury. He is therefore a truly objective observer: with no commitment to the past, he can have no commitment to the future. And since he is uncommitted, he is an ideal listener to the troubles and schemes of Mrs. Beverly Guinevere's boarders in Brooklyn Heights.

Lovett, lonely and confused, drifts into a friendship with Guinevere's husband, a former official of the Soviet International who is living as a boarder under the name of

4. Norman Mailer, *The Presidential Papers* (New York: Putnam, 1963), p. 136. This interview with Paul Krassner is abridged from *The Realist*, No. 40 (December 1962), 1, 13–16, 18–23, 10.

5. The two quotations in this paragraph are from Norman Mailer, *Advertisements for Myself* (New York: Putnam, 1959), p. 106 and p. 94.

McLeod. Another boarder, LeRoy Hollingsworth, has been assigned by the U.S. government to recover a secret which McLeod is suspected of stealing (after his defection from the Soviets McLeod worked for the U.S. government). Assisting Hollingsworth is Lannie Madison, who seeks revenge because she holds McLeod partly responsible for the death of the idol of her youth, Trotsky. These relationships and personal histories are not made explicit in the manner of *The Naked and the Dead*, but are revealed gradually and artfully through the eyes of the narrator as he discovers them. And some points, like the identity of the "little object" McLeod is suspected of stealing, are left purposely ambiguous.

There is little doubt that Mailer intended his characters to be representative of certain types in modern society. Lovett is the sensitive intellectual, cut off from his heritage of the past, anxious and uncertain about the future, searching for personal relationships and political beliefs to which he can commit himself. He finally makes this commitment by becoming a disciple of McLeod, a commitment to guard the heritage of socialist tradition until its phoenix-like resurrection from the ashes of the final war. It is Lovett who inherits the "little object" in the end. Although its identity is never revealed (Hollingsworth is not even authorized by his superior to know what he is looking for), the object may be, simply, hope.[6]

McLeod is the ex-Communist, disillusioned by the betrayal of the Revolution and ashamed of his own part in that betrayal. His belief in the importance of the Communist ends had overcome his revulsion at the means, and had led him to commit acts, such as the murder of deviationists, which he now knows were inexcusable. He is now pursued not only by the government, but even more relentlessly by his own conscience. Like Lovett, he is alienated from humanity, but for different reasons. McLeod had seen people not as human beings, but as tools to be manipulated in the development of the socialist state. It is only at the very end of his life that he

6. At the end of the book Lovett says "So the heritage passed on to me, poor hope, and the little object as well, and I went out into the world."

becomes capable of the "selfless friendship" which he discovers to be the only truly worthwhile human relationship. But by then it is too late.

Lannie is the remote idealist, driven by a hostile world into psychosis, into "fathomless desperation." She drinks compulsively, as if from some deep urge to destroy herself. Although she permits Lovett to make love to her and Hollingsworth to degrade her sexually, she seeks and enjoys sex only with Guinevere. Life, she tells Lovett, is a prison which we must choose to enter, and choose gladly. She often dreams of a mouse who is Christ, and she herself feels compelled to share the suffering of others and to seek it for herself.

Guinevere, faithless queen of the boardinghouse, is the twentieth-century mob personified. Her values are the values of Hollywood, where she claims to have slept around and where she dreams of sending her daughter Monina. She is ready to sell out her husband to Hollingsworth, with whom she plans to run away, and at the same time she is teasing Lovett and discovering new forms of sexual ecstasy with Lannie. Her sex life is symbolic of her life in general: selfish, grasping, mindless, animalistic.

Hollingsworth, the government representative in the boardinghouse, is also selfish, materialistic, dominated by the pleasure principle. He can achieve sexual satisfaction only by inflicting pain (as with Guinevere) or degradation (as with Lannie). He is the eminently practical man who can recognize his own inadequacies without allowing them to tear him apart. He is interested only in facts, and is contemptuous of theory and feeling; he is well qualified to build the government's case against McLeod. "I don't give two cents for all your papers," he tells McLeod and Lovett. "A good-time Charley, that's myself, and that's why I'm smarter than the lot of you."

Whether or not Hollingsworth is smarter, he wins in the end. He kills McLeod and carries off the fair Guinevere. Although *Barbary Shore* is not an entirely systematic allegory, its implications are clear enough: the crowd has been seduced by totalitarianism, and the liberal cause has been fragmented and driven underground. In retrospect, the novel appears to be remarkably prophetic of the McCarthy era and the deepening schizophrenia of the cold war. Hollingsworth objectifies what Hannah Arendt has called the banality of evil; he is a modern American Eichmann, doing his duty unquestioningly and competently for a modest reward. Throughout the novel McLeod and Lovett and Lannie are unable to deal with him effectively because they live in a different moral dimension; their ideals and theories and consciences are simply irrelevant to Hollingsworth. Guinevere, like Hollingsworth, is not troubled by morality; she merely connives and submits. And in Mailer's scheme of things, she represents the American masses.

In Lovett, however, Mailer does seem to present a muted hope. It is Lovett who finally inherits the "little object" and who plans to use it in the service of humanity. As the story develops he recovers fragments of his past; significantly, most of his new-found memories are of love. Although these memories are of "profane" love, he is also shown to be moving toward the "selfless friendship" which McLeod had spoken of, and which apparently will be the key to Lovett's possible salvation and to his possible salvation of others. The last paragraphs of the book summarize Lovett's final point of view:

So the heritage passed on to me, poor hope, and the little object as well, and I went out into the world. If I fled down the alley which led from that rooming house, it was only to enter another, and then another. I am obliged to live waiting for the signs which tell me I must move on again.

Thus, time passes, and I work and I study, and I keep my eye on the door.

Meanwhile, vast armies mount themselves, the world revolves, the traveller clutches his breast. From out the unyielding contradictions of labor stolen from men, the march to the endless war forces its pace. Perhaps, as the millions will be lost, others will be created, and I shall discover brothers where I thought none existed.

But for the present the storm approaches its thunderhead, and it is apparent that the boat drifts ever closer to shore. So the blind will lead the blind, and the deaf shout warnings to one another until their voices are lost.

The image of the drifting voyager recurs throughout the book. In the first chapter Lovett describes a frequently recurring dream in which a traveler returning home in a taxi through the streets of his native city suddenly finds everything unfamiliar. The traveler, horrified and afraid that he is dreaming, allows the cab to go on and on, while Lovett shouts to him that "this city is the real city, the material city, and your vehicle is history." But the traveler cannot hear him. And the final sentence of this chapter states the theme which will be echoed by the final sentence of the book: "So the blind lead the blind and the deaf shout warnings to one another until their voices are lost."

The frail vessel of civilization is drifting helplessly down upon the Barbary shore. Why Barbary? The answer is given by Guinevere, who has asked Hollingsworth to take her away with him. When he asks her where she wants to go, she replies "Anywhere. To the ends of the earth. To Barbary—I like the sound of that." Anywhere. The sickness of our society, Mailer is saying, is mindless and cannot be treated rationally. Society is in peril not from the wrong ideas, but from the lack of interest in any ideas at all. It has become a great Guinevere—fat, stupid, faithless, obsessed with its own sensual gratification. Although voices, like those of McLeod and Lovett (and even the mad shrieks of Lannie), cry out our peril, Guinevere cannot hear them: the voices speak a foreign language. And in the din of "civilization" these voices are mere murmurs; as McLeod points out, such voices "in sufficient numbers and with sufficient passion and consciousness . . . will never exist. If they do not, however, then the human condition is incapable of alleviation, and we can only witness for a century at least and perhaps forever the disappearance of all we have created." Mailer is doubtful whether enough voices like Lovett's will ever be heard, but he leaves the possibility open.

In *Barbary Shore* Mailer goes much deeper into the psychic origins of behavior than in *The Naked and the Dead*. Although his characters are not presented primarily in sexual terms as they are in much of his later work, their sexual natures are central; they involve, describe, and perhaps even define the whole nature of the individual. And the allegorical nature of *Barbary Shore* extends this involvement to include society as a whole.

Lovett, the contemporary liberal, is cut off from his social heritage by amnesia. He is also adrift sexually; his sexual meaning is lost in his forgotten past. In the present he is teased by Guinevere, the living symbol of empty sensuality. His brief sexual involvement with Lannie is a measure of her "fathomless despair" and an indication of Lovett's own incompletion.

McLeod, the ex-Communist, also illustrates this fragmentary, incomplete nature. His view of life is theoretical. His love for Guinevere is greater than he consciously admits, but it fails because his attempts at reconciliation with her are intellectual and verbal, in a language foreign to the sensuality which she understands. And McLeod does not understand her language either; he does not realize until too late that existence must be sensual as well as intellectual. In his relations with her and the others there seems to be a strong sexual element which he is not aware of. His interest in Lovett's progress with Guinevere, for example, is more than the intellectual curiosity which he professes. And it is possible that his need for confession is partly a sexual need; it certainly reflects a need for some sort of emotional involvement.

Lannie, like McLeod, is haunted by her feelings of guilt for the death of Trotsky. And like McLeod, she feels a perverse need for martyrdom. She seeks sex as a form of punishment and gets a strange pleasure from her sexual degradation. Her sexual relations with Lovett, Hollingsworth, and Guinevere all reflect this psychic need for pain and punishment. The psychic natures of Lannie and McLeod, dominated by guilt complexes, are easily exploited by Hollingsworth.

Hollingsworth and Guinevere, dominated by the id or pleasure principle, objectify the political and social psychology of the masses: their only criterion for choice is self-gratification. The personality of Guinevere is carried to its logical and horrifying extreme in her daughter Monina, who is, as Harris Dienstfrey has pointed out, "obviously a token of the generation to come, a child of the mass media as Mailer sees them. Hardly able to speak, she is nevertheless a consummate narcissist, brilliantly aware of the most delicate sexual nuance. . . . She lives in fantasy and emerges into the real world only to be shocked into fright." [7]

Although *Barbary Shore* was compared unfavorably to *The Naked and the Dead* by most reviewers, it is a much deeper, more fascinating, and less mechanical book. Its apocalyptic, compelling vision is reminiscent of D. H. Lawrence. And perhaps the most compelling aspect of *Barbary Shore* is the tension created between the objective and the psychic levels of the story, between the events themselves and their buried psychic meanings. Mailer himself was aware of this tension:

My conscious intelligence . . . became obsessed by the Russian Revolution. But my unconscious was much more interested in other matters: murder, suicide, orgy, psychosis, all the themes I discuss in *Advertisements*. Since the gulf between these conscious and unconscious themes was vast and quite resistant to any quick literary coupling, the tension to get a bridge across resulted in the peculiar feverish hothouse atmosphere of the book. My unconscious felt one kind of dread, my conscious mind another, and *Barbary Shore* lives somewhere between. That's why its focus is so unearthly.[8]

A somewhat similar focus is used in *The Deer Park* (1955), which is more realistic than *Barbary Shore*, though it is set in Guinevere's land of dreams. According to Mailer, the book was begun as the first of a series of eight novels whose themes would provide a panorama of contemporary American life,[9] but he abandoned the idea after finishing the first draft of *The Deer Park*.

The theme of the first novel was to be "pleasure." The ac-

7. Harris Dienstfrey, "The Fiction of Norman Mailer," in Richard Kostelanetz (ed.), *On Contemporary Literature* (New York: Avon, 1964), p. 427.
8. *Paris Review* interview, p. 40.
9. The eight themes were to be: "pleasure, business, communism, church, working class, crime, homosexuality, and mysticism" (Mailer, *Advertisements*, p. 154).

tion takes place mostly in Desert D'Or, a fictional Palm Springs, where the veterans of the Hollywood wars come for rest and rehabilitation. His narrator is Sergius O'Shaughnessy, who has come to Desert D'Or from another war, and for special rehabilitation. Like Lovett of *Barbary Shore*, Sergius is an outsider. Lovett had lost his past; Sergius is trying to lose his—a series of napalm missions he had flown against Korean villages. For him, as for Lovett, "everything is in the present tense," and he is caught in the familiar existential dilemma: "I knew that finally one most do, simply do, for we act in total ignorance and yet in honest ignorance we must act, or we can never learn for we can hardly believe what we are told, we can only measure what has happened inside ourselves." From Hearn to Lovett to Sergius is thus a progression from external to internal choices and justifications.

The therapeutic "good time" which Sergius is looking for proves to be illusory. Although he regains his sexual confidence with the movie star Lulu Meyers, their affair eventually becomes as meaningless as the liaisons in the Deer Park of Louis XV, which Mailer's epigraph suggests as an archetypal Palm Springs. The movie industry, the furthest development of Guinevere's American dream, is fraudulent: it sells a phony product to a gullible public. Supreme Pictures produces not the deep, disquieting truths of art, but the shallow, comforting half-truths of mass entertainment. Lulu, a love goddess on the screen, is wholly narcissistic in private life. The popular leading man of Supreme Pictures, Teddy Pope, is a blatant homosexual. The head of the studio, Herman Teppis, moralizes in public but deals savagely with his employees. *The Deer Park* is a sweeping, savage indictment of the schizophrenic world of Hollywood, where every glowing public personality masks a dark, grasping, vicious inner self. In their frantic pursuit of pleasure and power, these personalities only sink deeper into schizophrenia. In Hollywood, Mailer shows, illusions have become institutionalized, and hypocrisy has become a way of life. Success in the Hollywood jungle demands total acceptance of its jungle morality.

But there are some whose sense of personal integrity makes the cost of acceptance seem too high. Charles Francis Eitel,

Sergius' idol, is a director who had refused to cooperate with a witch-hunting Congressional committtee and had consequently been blacklisted by the industry. Eitel finally capitulates to the committee and ascends in the Supreme hierarchy once more. The financial and social pressures upon him, however, are not the real reasons for his surrender. His first appearance before the committee had been, in a sense, an empty gesture, the futile assertion of an integrity which he had already lost. He had already sold out too often in countless small ways; now in exile in Desert D'Or, he finds that he cannot write the honest script he had always wanted to. His years of shallow success have killed his ability to create the art which he still believes in. "Life has made me a determinist," he says, but this is only his final, despairing rationalization.

The cast of the novel ranges from Herman Teppis, the utterly corrupt head of Supreme Pictures, to the lowliest hangers on. Of major importance, however, are three characters in addition to Eitel and Sergius: Elena Esposito, a dancer who is kept by several men and finally married by Eitel; Marion Faye, a pimp; and Lulu Meyers, a movie star.

Lulu loves the movies; stardom sustains her. Leaving a party at four in the morning, she is besieged by autograph seekers. Their adulation feeds her ego: "isn't this a wonderful life?" she remarks. Her career comes first, before any human considerations, such as her love for Sergius. When she has to choose between remaining with him and returning to Hollywood, for example, her choice is instinctive.

Elena is more generous, more perceptive, more honest, more sensitive than Lulu. Her openness places her at a disadvantage in the modern Deer Park; because she keeps nothing in reserve to bargain with, she is at the mercy of her lovers. Eitel recognizes and admires this in her, and finally marries her out of pity, when it becomes evident that she has exhausted her emotional resources. Her suffering has not hardened her, but made her more sensitive. It is the courage of her refusal to protect herself by withdrawing which attracts Eitel most of all.

Marion Faye, to whom Elena turns when her affair with

Eitel goes sour, has grown bitter; his sense of outrage at the phoniness of Desert D'Or has led him to feel only contempt for the victims of the golden wasteland: "Faye knew all about compassion. It was the worst of the vices; he had learned that a long time ago . . . once you knew that guilt was the cement of the world, there was nothing to it; you could own the world or spit at it. But first you had to get rid of your own guilt, and to do that you had to kill compassion." Faye's stable of call girls serves the pleasures of the affluent movie makers. With the girls and their clients he explores the depths of the unconscious, where he seeks the roots of our modern schizophrenia. It is these depths, he feels, which govern what we are and do, but they have no acknowledged place in the pollyanna philosophy which prevails in Hollywood, and indeed in the nation as a whole. The first step in therapy, Faye feels, is to see these depths as they really are.

Faye's answer is that to live in a rotten world, one must become rotten. If the world is a whore, then Faye will be her pimp. Under the influence of marijuana, his vision is frequently transformed from sexual to religious imagery: "For beyond, in the far beyond, was the heresy that God was the Devil and the One they called the Devil was God-in-banishment like a noble prince deprived of true heaven, and God who was the Devil had conquered heaven, and God who was the Devil had conquered except for the few who saw the cheat that God was not God at all. So he prayed, 'Make me cold, Devil, and I will run the world in your name.'"

And the religious theme, in turn, invades the world of sex: Faye the pimp and Elena his mistress became Father Faye the flagellant monk and Sister Elena the lewd nun. Faye's morbid, and nearly successful, desire to make Elena kill herself seems to represent an almost religious form of protest. For Faye is the prophet and priest of Armageddon: "So let it come, Faye thought, let this explosion come, and then another, and all the others, until the Sun God burned the earth. Let it come, he thought, looking into the east at Mecca [Los Alamos] where the bombs ticked. . . . Let it come, Faye begged, like a man praying for rain, let it come and clear the rot and the stench and the stink, let it come for all of everywhere, just so it comes and the world stands clear in the white dead dawn."

Faye's apocalyptic vision is close to Mailer's own. He sees the world of Hollywood as the symbolic sum of all of America's illusions. *The Deer Park* shows that those illusions are ultimately intolerable and unsatisfying. But there are only two routes out of Hollywood—either toward the truth or further into an even more illusory existence, such as the world of Desert D'Or. Sergius, Faye, and Elena, involved as they are with the world of illusion, nevertheless make their conscious commitment to truth. Lulu, despite her frequent awareness of truth, is committed to the world of Supreme Pictures.

Eitel, the tragic hero of the novel (Faye is the existential hero), begins with an essential commitment to the truth, which he maintains at tremendous personal cost in his conflicts with the Congressional committee and with Supreme Pictures. But he finds that these conflicts and the compromises which he has made with the illusory world have taken too much out of him. His final surrender to that world is a tragic defeat, incurred in the full knowledge of its meaning and personal consequences. After years of creating cheap illusions for the Guineveres of this world, Eitel finds that he no longer knows how to tell the truth; and he is doomed to a posthumous life, to go on creating lies without even the hope, now, of creating anything better. His latest film, *Saints and Lovers*, had been conceived in truth but is now perverted by the phony religious morality marketed by Hollywood (the title itself, in fact, may be a perversion of Lawrence's *Sons and Lovers*).

Washington, superficially quite different from Hollywood, is still the other pole defining the illusory world of *The Deer Park*. The Congressional committee of superpatriots certifies the Americanism of the movie colony; dissenters are blacklisted. Mailer's story, of course, reflects the real story of the House Un-American Activities Committee and the entertainment industry during the McCarthy era. Like the real story, Mailer's is not comforting: it includes the principles of guilt by association, conviction for refusal to "cooperate," secret accusations, intimidation and harrassment of witnesses, and various other extralegal and illegal procedures. The point here, as in *Barbary Shore*, is the insidiousness of totalitarianism. One small compromise or concession leads to the next, until the situation reaches the dimensions of unconditional surrender—the status which Eitel finally reaches. He cannot survive in "Hollywood without accepting its demands, and ultimately these demands—both artistic and political—are total.

As Mailer had suggested in *The Naked and the Dead* and implied more strongly in *Barbary Shore*, these demands are psychic in origin. The villains of *The Deer Park*, like those of the earlier work, are driven by the pleasure principle. Hollywood, like Hamlet's Denmark, is sick with greed and sensuality. Herman Teppis, king of Supreme Pictures, is its ruthless, subtle, and absolute ruler. Like Hollingsworth of *Barbary Shore*, Teppis sees people as objects. To raise Lulu's sagging popularity, he plans to marry her to Teddy Pope, a homosexual leading man. And he sees Bobby, an aspiring actress, simply as a "frightened female mouth, facsimile of all those smiling lips he had seen so ready to serve at the thumb of power." The phallic power of Teppis, apparently impotent except in the frightened female mouth, is symbolic of the sickness of his kingdom of illusions. Even Lulu, who restores Sergius' lost phallic power, must use him; she insists that they act out roles in their lovemaking, and she likes nothing better than to talk to Teppis on the telephone at the same time. For Sergius, their affair becomes an athletic endurance contest.

A difficulty in *The Deer Park* which is often noticed, and which Mailer himself has admitted, is the conception of the narrator. Unfortunately, Sergius is the least convincing character in the novel. Although we are told a great deal about him, we seldom really see him. And he does not function as an effective "lens" for the interpretation of the other characters; large sections of the book, concerned entirely with other characters and supposedly reconstructed by the narrator, strain the credibility of Mailer's narrative technique.

Yet Sergius does serve several useful purposes in *The Deer Park*. As an outsider he gives us a more objective view than an insider could. His past also serves as an indirect indictment of American inhumanity abroad; our foreign policy in the Far East is shown to suffer from the same schizophrenia which the novel illustrates on the domestic scene. But Sergius seems most important as a philosophical character who is forced to choose between the extremes objectified by Eitel and Faye. In the conflict between liberalism and Hipsterism, Sergius leans toward the latter—though Mailer shows that neither extreme is viable in the modern world. The tolerance and compassion of liberalism, as Faye recognizes, are crippling; Eitel's integrity is eroded by pity—not only pity for others, which hurts them unnecessarily (Elena and Bobby, for example), but pity for himself. Faye tries to become ruthless and uncompromising, contemptuous of the weak, the helpless, the defeated. But in doing so, he dehumanizes himself too, so that he approaches the character of Teppis. In the final chapter, an epilogue, Sergius imagines a valedictory message from the defeated Eitel, counselling "defiance" in his art. But Sergius remains convinced of the value of a good time, since that "is what gives us the strength to try again." And then Sergius imagines himself asking God

"Would You agree that sex is where philosophy begins?"
But God who is the oldest of the philosophers, answers in His weary cryptic way, "Rather think of Sex as Time, and Time as the connection of new circuits."

And on that cryptic note the novel ends, with the philosophical questions unresolved.

Yet Sergius' notion about sex as the beginning of philosophy indicates a leaning toward Faye's, rather than Eitel's position. And the excerpts from Mailer's work in progress in *Advertisements for Myself*, as well as his statements about that work, show that this was Mailer's own point of view. In "The Man Who Studied Yoga," which is the prologue to the projected series of eight novels, the themes of the projected work are introduced. The prologue, related by an anonymous and omniscient narrator, is focused upon Sam Slovoda, a former radical who is now a writer for the comic strips. Slovoda, now undergoing analysis with a Dr. Sergius, is contemplating a novel which will capture the essence of modern experience, but his conception of the book is blocked by his sense that "reality is no longer realistic," and that the traditional approaches to fiction are inadequate to express an experience of life which is schizoid.

He and his wife Eleanor have some friends in for the evening to watch a pornographic movie. Each viewer becomes engrossed in the sexual fantasy being acted on the screen, and for a moment Sam wonders whether the movie may lead to an orgy. But he knows that the group will feel compelled to dominate the situation intellectually. And it does: the party ends with an analysis of the movie. After the friends leave Sam and Eleanor watch the movie again, make love in front of it, and afterwards, analyze the experience, concluding that it "has been good but not quite right." The response to the movie, both by the group as a whole and by the couple, has been Eitel's rather than Faye's. The film has revealed what Teppis had called the monster in the heart of man. But the response to the monster had been purely intellectual—and therefore false. An orgy would have been more honest.

The plan for which "The Man Who Studied Yoga" is the prologue was abandoned after Mailer had written the first draft of The Deer Park. But in Advertisements he presents three excerpts from an even more ambitious work. The excerpts are the prologue, a poem, and an episode called "The Time of Her Time." The narrator of the new prologue is, like the earlier narrator, an amorphous, choric presence concerned with the nature of his own being as well as with the nature of his characters in his journey "from the consciousness of one being to the emotions of another." Although endowed with god-like powers, the narrator is baffled by the nature of God:

So I approach Him, if I have not already lost Him, God, in His destiny, in which He may succeed, or tragically fail, for God like Us suffers the ambition to make a destiny more extraordinary than was conceived for Him, yes God is like Me, only more so.
Unless—spinning instead through the dark of some inner Space—

the winds are icy here—I do no more than delude myself, fall back into that hopeless odyssey where libido never lingers, and my nature is nothing other than to search for the Devil while I carry with me the minds of some of you.

This meditation, which closes the prologue, reflects what appears to be the primary theme of Mailer's recent work.

From the prologue we learn that the scene is a house near Provincetown owned by Faye (now a millionaire) in which a Negro madame is giving a party, and that Faye is to be one of the three "heroes" of the novel. The other two heroes are a "television celebrity and a psychoanalyst" who are later identified as "Shawn Sergius (born perhaps as Sergius O'Shaughnessy), the only creative personality ever to dominate television, and Dr. Joyce, the psychoanalyst, who became so overextended beyond his humane means, and had so compromised his career, his profession, and his intimate honor that he was contemplating suicide long before he came to the party." A list of some four dozen categories into which the guests fit is given, and the narrator then gives a tantalizing hint of the revelry to come, which includes murder and suicide.

The "connection" of sex and time suggested in the closing paragraphs of *The Deer Park* is discussed by the madame and a physicist in the prologue. She advances a theory of time as either "potential" or "dynamic." It is potential or passive when "it doesn't connect"; this, says the narrator, is "Time on its way to death": it is "onanistic" and "remains in step to the twitching of a clock." Time becomes dynamic when it is "excited into action" by murder or love, which break the onanistic spiral and move us toward the future. The narrator, uncertain of his own nature and destiny, also reveals an obsession with time:

But now I go, the vortex does not stop, the winds of the whirlpool—God's gyre again?—are heavy with consequence, and I sink or do I fly? all vectors gone, while in my center, clear as the icy eye of cocaine, I race toward a point of judgment, my courage and my cowardice (my masculine thrust and retreat from the avaricious energy-plucking hairy old grotto of Time) trailing behind me in that comet of connotations which is the past topologically reversed by the vision of *now*, as if in recovering the past I am chasing after the future, so that the past, the net of the name-giving surface-perceiving past, is my future again, and I go out into the past, into the trail of the cold eye of past relationship, the eye of my I at home in the object-filled chaos of any ego I choose, at least for this short while between the stirrup and the ground, for in an instant—will it be eternally long? like some cell at the crisis of its cellvish destiny, I race into the midnight mind, the dream-haunted determinations of that God of whom I was a part, and will He choose me to be born again? have I proved one of his best? am I embryo in some belly of the divisible feminine Time, or is the journey yet to make? Or worst of all am I?—and the cry which is without sound shrieks in my ears—am I already on the way out? a fetor of God's brown sausage in His time of diarrhea, oozing and sucking and bleating like a fecal puppy about to pass away past the last pinch of the divine sphincter with only the toilet of Time, oldest hag of them all, to spin me away into the spiral of star-lit empty waters.

"God's gyre" reminds us of Yeats. In an *Esquire* column reprinted in *The Presidential Papers* Mailer has spoken of "The Second Coming" as "the best short poem of the twentieth century." It is the qualities of courage and coward-ice, Mailer seems to be saying, which offer us the possibility of salvation from the warm womb of inevitable defeat. The rough beast of which Yeats wrote in "The Second Coming" can be an apocalyptic redeemer. In Mailer's view, acqui-escence is the cardinal sin of our time: in it we become mechanical, onanistic, fecal. But with courage man can break the lifeless, narrowing spiral which is the past endlessly re-peating itself. The past can be "topologically reversed by the vision of *now*" if we have the will, the courage, and the strength.

This passage also illustrates, probably better than any other, Mailer's new organic prose style. It is a series of stunning sensory impressions, quite unlike the expository style of *The Naked and the Dead*. From the earlier fidelity to the rhythms of everyday speech he has moved to a new synthesis of rhythm, sound, and emotional tones and overtones. The words are loaded with emotional as well as literal meaning, and with their vivid evocations of sounds, smells, tactile feel-ings, and motions—as well as the more conventional visual images—Mailer achieves an almost overwhelming sense of the psychological totality of his situation. It is this new style, more than any other factor (except perhaps for Mailer's shrill insistence on the scatological) which has provoked so much hostility to his recent work. Many readers apparently expect him to continue to play by the rules with which he began. But writers who set out to abrogate all the rules must make up their own as they go along.

Mailer's recent sexual theories are illustrated in "The Time of Her Time." The narrator, who may be Sergius O'Shaugh-nessy, is in the unlikely business of operating a school for bullfighters in Greenwich Village. Essentially, the episode is the graphic account of the three nights which the narrator needs to bring a nineteen-year-old Jewish coed to her first orgasm. The girl typifies the younger New York "in" group; she is a victim of the "gyre" of sterile intellectuality which Mailer sees as the sickness of our time. She tells the narrator that she and her steady boyfriend practice "the oral per-versions. That's because, vaginally, I'm anaesthetized—a good phallic narcissist like you doesn't do enough for me." This is typical of her small talk; she finds meaning not in experience itself, but in the analysis of it. On the final night, through his instinctive sexual art, which includes sodomy and the words "You dirty little Jew" spoken at just the right moment, the exhausted narrator brings her to her first therapeutic orgasm. Ironically, the experience is almost entirely mechanical for him—as sex in Mailer's work invariably is. The narrator is emotionally detached, playing a coldly calculated game of sexual chess, constantly analyzing his opponent's moves, strengths, and weaknesses, devising his strategy for victory. Ironically also, the lovers part as enemies; the time of her time is fleeting, and the connection is broken again.

The other excerpt from the work in progress is a poem en-titled "Dead Ends," written by a rich homosexual "in vision of his unrequited love for Marion." Its thesis is that men become homosexual to save themselves from cancer. This view is ap-

parently close to Mailer's own, expressed several times elsewhere, that cancer is the psychosomatic disease of our time,
related somehow to our failure to fight the mass psychosis of
contemporary life. "Narcissism," says the poet, "is the cause
of cancer." It is the disease of passive time,

> For what we do not dare to feel
> returns then as waste and routine
> to the depths of the flesh. . . .

The first installment of a new novel by Mailer appeared in
Esquire in January, 1964. Nine years had passed since the
publication of *The Deer Park*, and the new work was awaited
with considerable curiosity. Mailer's career in those nine years
seemed to be the record of a large talent fragmented and
largely wasted in journalism and in the few impressive but
apparently abortive attempts at a vast new work which had
appeared in *Advertisements*. Would the new book fulfill that
promise, or would it be another piece of exciting journalism?
Critical response to the novel in its serialized form tended
toward the second of these alternatives, and even in its re-
vised book form *An American Dream* (1965) has had a
mixed reception. Some critics have refused to take it seriously, preferring to regard it as sensational "pop fiction" ex-
ploiting sex, sadism, and violence.

Undeniably, the book is sensational. Its hero, Stephen
Richards Rojack, is a Harvard man (Phi Beta Kappa, *summa
cum laude*), war hero, ex-Congressman, friend of President
Kennedy, "professor of existential psychology" at a metropolitan university in New York, and husband of an heiress,
the former Deborah Kelly, whom he had met on a double date
with Kennedy when the two men were freshman Congress-
men.

Rojack claims to have "stolen" Deborah from Kennedy.
Shortly after the double date, which had ended with Deborah and Rojack spending the night in the back seat of his car,
she had entered a convent. Nine years later she had left the
order and married him in Paris. But their marriage had been

an adventure in psychological warfare, and at the time the novel opens they are separated. In the first chapter Rojack visits her apartment; when she taunts him with an account of her latest love affairs, he strikes her, they struggle, and she is killed.

Rojack enjoys the killing, and in a state of euphoria he decides that Deborah's "grace" has passed to him, that he has killed her evil. He decides not to call the police, but guided by the "magic" which inspires his most existential actions, he walks unannounced into the room of Ruta, Deborah's German maid. He finds her masturbating, and in a scene reminiscent of "The Time of Her Time" he gives her what she needs. When he returns to Deborah's room he decides to make her death look like suicide and pushes her body out the window of the tenth-floor apartment. He then calls the police and stops to make love to Ruta in the hall on his way out to the street, where he mourns over Deborah's body.

The police are suspicious of his story and take him in for questioning, but release him temporarily for lack of evidence. He then goes to a private club where he practices the telepathic power with which the killing has endowed him. The blonde singer, Cherry, gets his message, and they go to her apartment. She had been the mistress of Deborah's father, who had taken her to Las Vegas with him but had lost interest when she had become pregnant; then she had fallen in love with Shago Martin, a Negro musician, who also got her pregnant. Both pregnancies had ended in abortions. Rojack the sexual therapist brings her to her first orgasm. Their idyll is interrupted by Shago, who threatens Rojack with a knife, and Rojack beats him badly.

Just when Rojack is getting really worried, the police are ordered to dismiss their case against him. Rojack surmises that Kelly has been responsible for this and goes to see him in his apartment in the Waldorf Towers. Ruta opens the door; it turns out that she had been spying on Deborah for Kelly. In the library the two men talk; Kelly discovers that Rojack had killed Deborah, and Rojack discovers that Kelly had seduced her when she was fifteen and had then continued the affair. On the balcony of the apartment Rojack feels he must prove something by walking around the parapet, four hundred feet above the street. Through a tremendous effort of will, he almost succeeds. Kelly, who senses Rojack's victory, attempts to knock him off the parapet, but Rojack regains the balcony and knocks Kelly unconscious.

On his way out of the apartment Rojack has the feeling that he must make the journey around the parapet again; he senses somehow that Cherry's life is in the balance. But he goes instead to her apartment, where the police meet him with the news that Shago has been killed in Morningside Park and Cherry has been brutally beaten in her apartment. Just then the stretcher emerges; Cherry tells him that she is going to die, and she does.

The Epilogue finds Rojack in Las Vegas. On his way, he had stopped in Missouri and witnessed an autopsy, and the stench of the putrescent corpse had stayed with him for days. Now he is using his psychic powers at the gambling tables, building up a stake for a further journey. On the eve of his departure he drives along a deserted road in the desert and stops at an abandoned telephone booth. He dials the phone and asks for Cherry. She tells him that "the girls are swell. Marilyn says to say hello," and to "keep the dice for free, the moon is out and she's a mother to me." Although he thinks of calling her again, Rojack says, "in the morning I was something like sane again," and he leaves for Guatemala and Yucatan.

This summary indicates something of the wild improbability of *An American Dream*. It is evident, of course, from the first sentence ("I met Jack Kennedy in November, 1946") that we are not dealing with an ordinary realistic novel. And the title itself suggests that the book is not intended as realism. But whose dream is it? And what is it about?

Like Mailer's earlier fiction, *An American Dream* is panoramic in intent and scope: it is concerned with every conceivable aspect of American life—and maybe some which are inconceivable as well. If the book has any focus, however, it is on the psychic sources of power in the personality. It is in these psychic mysteries, rather than in philosophical or social theories, that Mailer is now searching for his "explanation" of human behavior and the human condition. And the starting point for the psychic exploration in the novel is Rojack himself; unlike the narrators of Mailer's earlier novels, Rojack is the central figure.

And Rojack, again unlike these earlier narrators, knows what he is looking for. His central obsession is "the not inconsiderable thesis that magic, dread, and the perception of death were the roots of motivation." Although Rojack does not define "magic," it seems to mean the psychic power which the existentialist achieves in his heroic confrontation with the absurd—an instinctive sense of what to do. "There's nothing but magic at the top," Kelly tells Rojack. Apparently incest was the key which unlocked the power of magic for Kelly, as murder becomes the key for Rojack. At any rate, the magic leads to a fortune for Kelly and to strange psychic powers for Rojack.

"Dread" Rojack defines as "the natural result of any invasion of the supernatural." He sees himself as acting on the side of God in the existential war against the Devil, and his own identity is imperiled by the possibility of God's defeat. "I would suppose existence ceased if God is destroyed," he tells Kelly. Kelly is aware of the war too, but is fighting on the other side. Speaking of his seduction of Deborah, he says that "to fail the promise of this extraordinary moment would deprive me of some indefinable potential." The struggle of Rojack and Kelly on the balcony, then, is symbolic of the existential war between God and the Devil. Neither wins; although Kelly is temporarily defeated, Rojack does not have the will to walk around the parapet again, and he fails Cherry, the corrupted innocent.

The third factor in Rojack's psychic equation, "the perception of death," is the ultimate fact which the existentialist must recognize. It seems to be symbolized in *An American Dream* by the moon, which illuminates Rojack's confrontations with death: his reckless attack upon the German machine gun nests in Italy, his impulse to plunge from the balcony in the opening chapter, his murder of Deborah, his struggle with Kelly, and his final conversation in the desert with Cherry. The air-conditioned chill of the motels and casinos of Las Vegas suggest to him "life in the safety chambers of the moon," and he "knew that the deserts of the West, the arid empty wild blind deserts, were producing again a new breed of man."

If Rojack is not of that new breed, he is at least a close forerunner. He is Mailer's white Negro, the Hipster or American existentialist, engaged in the violent conflict between God and the Devil, where the outcome is always conditional and where the fate of God as well as of the human protagonist hangs in the existential balance. As in Mailer's other work, the conflict has a vital sexual dimension. In the encounter with Ruta, for example, Rojack gives his phallic hostage alternately to "the Lord" and "Der Teufel." To Ruta's dismay, but to her delight too (she is a "Nazi," Rojack's instincts tell him, and therefore predisposed to sodomy), the Devil wins out. Throughout the novel in fact, sexual perversions (Rojack's with Ruta, Deborah's with her lovers, and her incest with her father) are associated with the Devil within us which continually threatens the forces of God in Mailer's cosmic conflict. *An American Dream* ends, like the earlier two novels, with the cosmic conflict unresolved, but with the narrator still committed to the good fight, still faithful to his instincts.

This analysis of Mailer's concept of the existential conflict between God and the Devil and his concept of an existential immortality may seem to be an extreme interpretation of his recent novels. And the novels themselves always suggest, rather than insist upon, these concepts. That they are indeed central to his philosophy, however, is borne out in his nonfiction.

Advertisements for Myself (1959) is an exceptionally frank and illuminating account of the development of Mailer's mind and career. This book reveals that Mailer recognized, and indeed had planned, the metamorphosis from disciple to prophet, from imitation of Dos Passos to the creation or at least the definition of a new American

Existentialism. Mailer had found his mission and had become convinced of its paramount importance: "I am imprisoned with a perception which will settle for nothing less than making a revolution in the consciousness of our time . . . it is my present and future work which will have the deepest influence of any work being done by an American novelist in these years."

The touchstone to Mailer's philosophy is the essay "The White Negro: Superficial Reflections on the Hipster," which first appeared in the Summer, 1957, issue of *Dissent* and which is reprinted in *Advertisements*. The White Negro [10] is

the American existentialist—the hipster, the man who knows that if our collective condition is to live with instant death by atomic war, relatively quick death by the State as *l'univers concentrationnaire,* or with a slow death by conformity with every creative and rebellious instinct stifled. . . , if the fate of twentieth-century man is to live with death from adolescence to premature senescence, why then the only life-giving answer is to accept the terms of death, to live with death as immediate danger, to divorce oneself from society, to live without roots, to set out on that uncharted journey into the rebellious imperatives of the self.

In a column for the *Village Voice* which preceded "The White Negro," Mailer had taken pains to dissociate Hip from "French existentialism" (which he never defines) by saying that "Hip is based on a mysticism of the flesh, and its origins can be traced back into all the undercurrents and underworlds of American life, back into the instinctive apprehension and appreciation of existence which one finds in the Negro and in the soldier, in the criminal psychopath and the dope addict and jazz musician, in the prostitute, in the actor, in the—if one can visualize such a possibility—in the marriage of the call-girl and the psychoanalyst." Apparently Mailer feels that "French existentialism" is primarily intellectual.

10. James Baldwin, "The Black Boy Looks at the White Boy," *Esquire,* LV, (May 1961), 102–106, attacks "The White Negro." Baldwin feels that Mailer maligns the Negroes in order to build his case for the Hipster. According to Baldwin the essay is built around the "myth of the sexuality of Negroes which Norman, like so many others, refuses to give up," p. 102.

The Hipster has much in common with the psychopath: both have an intuitive sense for action. While most of us are prisoners of habits and inhibitions, the psychopath and the Hipster live on the knife edge of violence, always ready to defeat fear by action. The psychopath, Mailer says, seeks love—love not in the socially acceptable forms, but in the form of the "apocalyptic orgasm." Life for the psychopath—and for the Hipster—has no past and no future, only the present moment, which contains all sensory experience. The present moment is dynamic rather than static, and the Hipster can either grow or wither at each moment. His objective, of course, is to grow—through new experiences, new insights. The key to growth is action; continued inaction is death. The most action, therefore the most growth, is to be found in violence. And the most love, the apocalyptic orgasm, is to be found there too.

Mailer does not dwell on the fact that the ultimate end of Hip is anarchy. The Hipster and the psychopath may be the Jekyll and Hyde of the twentieth century. But Mailer is too honest to ignore the possibility that Hipsters rather than conformists could destroy mankind. While he admits that the removal of all social restraints could lead to unprecedented violence, he nevertheless maintains that "man would then prove to be more creative than murderous and so would not destroy himself." This is a better risk, he says, than subscription to any of our current authoritarian philosophies or forms of government, in which the assumption is that man is inherently evil and that restraints are needed to save him from himself. These restraints, he feels, are themselves destroying man by denying "the necessity of life to become more than it has been." [11] The theme of *Advertisements for Myself*, he says, is that

---

11. George Steiner, "Naked But Not Dead," *Encounter*, XVII, vi (December 1961), 67–70, says of Mailer's philosophy of the Hipster and the "apocalyptic orgasm": "If we cut away the verbiage and the adolescent posturing in all this, there remains a doctrine of vehement candour and a bizarre yet compelling attempt to assert the sanctity of private life against the pressures of mass technocracy," p. 64.

the shits are killing us, even as they kill themselves—each day a few more lies eat into the seed with which we are born, little institutional lies from the print of newspapers, the shock waves of television, and the sentimental cheats of the movie screen. Little lies, but they pipe us toward insanity as they starve our sense of the real. We have grown up in a world more in decay than the worst of the Roman Empire, a cowardly world chasing after a good time (of which last one can approve) but chasing it without the courage to pay the hard price of full consciousness.

A keystone of the modern existential attitude is that the nature of reality, if reality does in fact have any systematic structure and coherence, is beyond the power of human perception. Mailer feels that "there are no truths other than tht isolated truths of what each observer feels at each instant of his existence."

Many existentialists, believing in isolated truths rather than a coherent and comprehensive truth, maintain that man must act rationally on the basis of his limited perceptions of these truths. Mailer, however, believes that man himself creates reality and that reality changes as man changes. The universe, he says, is "a changing reality whose laws are remade at each instant by everything living, but most particularly man, man raised to a neo-medieval summit where the truth is not what one has felt yesterday or what one expects to feel tomorrow but rather truth is no more nor less than what one feels at each instant in the perpetual climax of the present." In other words, reality is the instantaneous sum of all human attitudes toward reality; it is subjective and created by man rather than objective and perceived by man.

This definition of reality is the key to Mailer's very real and passionate belief in the possibility of social action. Reality can be transformed through the transformation of human attitudes toward it. The Hipster, in rejecting the prevailing social and moral restrictions, is creating a new society and a new morality which are relevant primarily to the self rather than to the social structure. According to Mailer, "The only Hip morality is to do what one feels whenever and wherever possible, and—this is how the war of the Hip and the Square begins—to be engaged in one primal battle: to open the limits of the possible for oneself, for oneself alone, because that is one's need." To open the limits of the possible, to make life more than it has been, is thus the criterion which must be used to judge every human action. Each man, Mailer says, is a "collection of possibilities, some more possible than others (the view of character implicit in Hip) and some humans are considered more capable than others of reaching more possibilities within themselves in less time, provided, and this is the dynamic, provided the particular character can swing at the right time."

Yet each decision, each action, must occur within a social context, and actions which are opposed to this context require far more energy than actions which are compatible with it. For this reason, actions which are compatible with the social context are more "possible," more likely, than actions which are incompatible. Confronted with many alternatives between growth and death, the Hipster must choose growth wherever he can, but he must also choose those alternatives on which to concentrate his energy.[12] Since there is never enough energy for all the alternatives, he must accept death in some in order to achieve growth in others. The danger is that he may be driven to desperation, like the psychopath, and may mistake death for growth, perhaps in some form of radical or reactionary political philosophy.

Mailer's Existentialism is transcendental. About a year after the publication of "The White Negro," Mailer first outlined his concept of God:

I think that the particular God we can conceive of is a god whose relationship to the universe we cannot divine; that is, how

12. Podhoretz quarrels with the motivation of Mailer's Hipster: "In my opinion, his great mistake is to attribute purpose and direction to the Hipster." Hipsterism, according to Podhoretz, "Norman Mailer: The Embattled Vision," 389, is "a symptom and not a significant protest, a spasmodic rather than an organized response." But Mailer throughout "The White Negro" shows the motivation of the Hipster as instinctual, and the "purpose and direction" of the Hipster is shown to arise from these instincts. Nevertheless, it is true that in the essay Mailer has constructed a rationale of Hipsterism and that his own philosophy reflects this rationale.

enormous He is in the scheme of the universe we can't begin to say. But almost certainly, He is not all-powerful; He exists as a warring element in a divided universe, and we are a part of—perhaps the most important part—of His great expression, His enormous destiny; perhaps He is trying to impose upon the universe His conception of being against other conceptions of being very much opposed to His. Maybe we are in a sense the seed, the seed-carriers, the voyagers, the explorers, the embodiment of that embattled vision; maybe we are engaged in a heroic activity, and not a mean one.

This concept was not a momentary pose. It is evident in *The Deer Park* and more explicit in *An American Dream*. It is most striking, perhaps, in a passage from *Advertisements* quoted earlier in this chapter (pp. 116–17), in which the narrator of Mailer's unfinished novel sees himself engaged in the service of an embattled God.

The Presidential Papers (1963) is a collection of Mailer's writing, primarily journalistic, since the publication of *Advertisements for Myself* in 1959. Ostensibly, the criterion for selection of these diverse pieces is that "their subject matter is fit concern for a President." In view of the wide scope of the President's concern, this criterion is not unduly restrictive.

To a reader familiar with the earlier work, *The Presidential Papers* offers only limited additional insight into Mailer's philosophy. It is valuable, however, in verifying and at times amplifying the material in the earlier work. It illustrates the application of these ideas to social situations, as, for example, in his analyses of the character of President Kennedy, the motives of juvenile gangs, the meaning of the reactionary movement in America, the nature of American politics.

Throughout the book Mailer deplores the tendency of modern society to restrict the range of human possibilities. America suffers, he says, from "a tyranny one breathed but could not define; it was felt as no more than a slow deadening of the best of our possibilities. . . ." And in commenting on the final lines of Yeats's "The Second Coming," (". . . What rough beast, its hour come round at last,/Slouches towards Bethlehem to be born?") Mailer recognizes the beast as "a shapeless force, an obdurate emptiness, an annihilation of possibilities."

As a result of this deadening of possibilities, the character of individual Americans is becoming submerged in the social character, which is growing increasingly false. American society is becoming permeated with "hypocrisies so elaborate they can no longer be traced." Most Americans instinctively recognize this falsity, and they are forced to lead a dual life—a surface life which is in harmony with the social hypocrisies, and an inner or "subterranean" life concerned with more real values: "Since the first World War Americans have been leading a double life, and our history has moved on two rivers, one visible, the other underground; there has been the history of politics which is concrete, factual, practical and unbelievably dull if not for the consequences of the actions of some of these men; and there is a subterranean river of untapped, ferocious, lonely and romantic desires, that concentration of ecstasy and violence which is the dream life of the nation."

This opening chasm between social and individual values is creating a national schizophrenia. Because the chasm has become so wide and deep, Americans are being increasingly compelled to choose either social or private values in order to preserve their sanity. Juvenile delinquency, Mailer thinks, is one symptom of this national schizophrenia. He recognizes in juvenile gangs the frantic search for positive values, for heightened individual possibilities: "courage, loyalty, honor and the urge for adventure."

Not only the juvenile delinquents, of course, are disillusioned with contemporary American society. In speaking of the dullness of the Eisenhower era, Mailer says, "the result was an alienation of the best minds and the bravest impulses from the faltering history which was made. America's need in those years was to take an existential turn, to walk into the nightmare. . . ." The existential turn, he had hoped, would be the election of Kennedy as President. The surface and underground values of American life had been nowhere farther apart than in politics, and in Kennedy—young, courageous, personable, dynamic, intelligent, informed, politically shrewd, and with a sense of history and tradition—Mailer sensed that

America had found a leader who could respond to the nation's deepest desires, an existential hero.[13] Mailer felt that "the life of politics and the life of myth had diverged too far," and he hoped that Kennedy would close the gap by creating a political reality which Americans could believe in and support.[14]

Mailer's campaign contribution appeared in *Esquire* for November, 1960, three weeks before Kennedy was elected, and Mailer feels that his article helped to swing the election by creating an aura of excitement about Kennedy which had not existed before among the intellectuals on the left. However, the political revolution which he had hoped for did not come about, and he feels that the hopes of the left have been dimmed by "the compromises and hypocrisies of a new Democratic administration."

America needs an existential hero, according to Mailer, because the human condition is existential. His definition of Existentialism stresses the finitude of the human intellect and faith in the perceptiveness, rightness, and power of human instincts: ". . . we live out our lives wandering among mysteries, and can construct the few hypotheses by which we guide ourselves only by drawing into ourselves the instinctive logic our inner voice tells us is true to the relations *between* mysteries. The separate mysteries we may never seize, but to appropriate a meaning from their relationship is possible." Existentialism, according to Mailer, is "the last of the humanisms."

In his earlier work, Mailer had suggested that anarchy, with

13. The title of the third Presidential Paper, which contains Mailer's campaign contributions to Kennedy, is "The Existential Hero."

14. Mailer's interest in politics has been continuous and well publicized. In 1948 he supported Henry Wallace for the presidency, and later ran for mayor of New York. According to the first sentence in *Advertisements for Myself*, "Like many another vain, empty, and bullying body of our time, I have been running for President these last ten years in the privacy of my mind . . .," 17. One reviewer took him literally; F. W. Dupee, "The American Norman Mailer," *Commentary*, XXIX (1960), 128–132, asks "Why, with a thousand-page novel to finish, does anyone *want* to be President, unless he fears that he will never finish the novel?" 130.

its possibilities for unlimited social violence, might be prefer-
able to a more comfortable but no less certain death—the
death of the individual soul by social strangulation. Now, however, he recognizes the necessity of laws: "I've never said
seriously that I'm an existential nihilist. I think I've said I'm
a constitutional nihilist, which is another matter. I believe all
legal structures are bad, but they've got to be dissolved with
art. I certainly wouldn't want to do away with all the laws
overnight."

According to Mailer, it is not the written laws so much as
the unwritten codes of values, morality, and behavior which
are responsible for the alienation of contemporary man from
society and from himself. These codes inhibit the possibilities
for the growth of character and for the discovery of self:

The logic in searching for extreme situations, in searching for
one's authenticity, is that one burns out the filament of old dull
habit and turns the conscious mind back upon its natural
subservience to the instinct. The danger of civilization is that its
leisure, its power, its insulation from nature, so alienate us from
instinct that our consciousness and our habits take on an autonomy
which may censor even the most necessary communication between
mind and instinct. For consciousness, once it is alienated from
instinct, begins to construct its intellectual formulations over a void.

Thus civilization encourages us to avoid the courageous encounter with nothingness which is the most necessary existential act.

Yet Mailer cannot really accept the ultimate encounter with
nothingness: death. As a matter of fact, he does not accept
nothingness itself, in the sense in which the existential
philosophers use the term—the absurd, or the possibility that
life may be meaningless. He says that

. . . the reluctance of modern European existentialism to take on
the logical continuation of the existential vision (that there is a life
after death which can be as existential as life itself) has brought
French and German existentialism to a halt on this uninhabitable
terrain of the absurd—to wit, man must lead his life as if death is
meaningful even when man *knows* that death is meaningless. This
revealed knowledge which Heidegger accepts as his working

hypothesis and Sartre goes so far as to assume is the certainty upon which he may build a philosophy, ends the possibility that one can construct a base for the existential ethic. The German philosopher runs aground trying to demonstrate the necessity for man to discover an authentic life. Heidegger can give no deeper explanation why man should bother to be authentic than to state in effect that man should be authentic in order to be free. Sartre's advocacy of the existential commitment is always in danger of dwindling into the minor aristocratic advocacy of leading one's life with style for the sake of style. Existentialism is rootless unless one dares the hypothesis that death is an existential continuation of life, that the soul may either pass through migrations, or cease to exist in the continuum of nature (which is the unspoken intimation of cancer). But accepting this hypothesis, authenticity and commitment return to the center of ethics, for man then faces no peril so huge as alienation from his own soul, a death which is other than death, a disappearance into nothingness rather than into Eternity.

To the thoughtful reader of Mailer's fiction, especially *The Deer Park*, and of his journalism, this insistence upon an "existential ethic" comes as no surprise. He has consistently maintained that the most crying need in America is for a system of values related to real human needs. His insistence upon immortality, however, as a concept necessary to give meaning to life would be regarded by Heidegger and Sartre as wishful thinking, an evasion of the facts of human existence. To Heidegger death, or the ever present possibility of death (and nothingness), is a condition of existence, a part of being; immortality would radically change the meaning of being. To Mailer the absurd may be uninhabitable terrain; to Sartre it is the only terrain—a battleground upon which man seizes meaning for his existence by exercising his freedom to choose and to act.

The Presidential Papers shows that the concept of metaphysical dualism in *Advertisements for Myself* and *An American Dream* is indeed central to Mailer's philosophy. This idea of a metaphysical war between good and evil is outlined again in a passage on the German concentration camps: "If God is not all-powerful but existential, discovering the possibilities and limitations of His creative powers in the form of the history which is made by His creatures, then one must postulate an existential equal to God, an antagonist, the Devil, a principle of Evil whose signature was the concentration camps, whose joy is to waste substance, whose intent is to prevent God's conception of Being from reaching its mysterious goal."

When Mailer says that "we were sent out of eternity to become more than we had been," he is dead serious. If God were omnipotent, man could have no real freedom. But man is free and "must," as Mailer said in his debate with William Buckley, "serve as God's agent" in the great metaphysical war whose battles are fought upon this earth, in the context of every present moment.

Mailer's most recent miscellany is *Cannibals and Christians* (1966), which features his classic polemic for *Esquire* on the Republican National Convention of 1964. Aside from this, the most interesting pieces in the volume are several "interviews" in which he expounds his theory of the existential conflict between God and the Devil and his theory of somatic psychology.

Mailer has come a long way since he decided, as a Harvard undergraduate, to write the great American novel of World War II. With a technique and an ideology inherited from the giants of the 1930's, he wrote a runaway best seller which many reviewers thought was that great novel. But Mailer was aware of the essential falsity of *The Naked and the Dead;* and, "imprisoned with a perception which will settle for nothing less than making a revolution in the consciousness of our time," he began to search far deeper beneath the surface of contemporary life to proclaim his message in a series of disturbing books. Although it is still too early to assess the results of Mailer's messianic mission, the nature of the mission itself is already apparent.

There is no reason to believe that Mailer has been influenced by D. H. Lawrence—beyond the general, inescapable influence that Lawrence has had upon the climate of our time. But in many ways Mailer's career has been reminiscent of Lawrence's. Both began well within the limits of traditional fiction, but developed an approach which was revolutionary, widely attacked, and only slowly understood. Both were concerned with the perversion of human life by the restrictions, false values, and hypocrisies of the social structure; and both moved beyond social criticism into a search for the psychic causes of social attitudes. Both became possessed by an apocalyptic vision of a new way of life, founded upon the recognition and acceptance of a truer concept of human nature, rising phoenix-like from the ashes of the old. Both were dedicated to creating a revolution in the consciousness of our time.

Revolutionaries like Lawrence and Mailer are seldom welcomed by the Establishment. Mailer's career is still developing; he is still searching for a synthesis which will explain to him the unique experience of our time. The beginning of such a synthesis is apparent in his central concept of the existential conflict between God and the Devil, between the forces which promise wider and deeper human possibilities and those which threaten to standardize and dehumanize man. It is possible, even likely, that Mailer will never achieve a satisfactory synthesis; his view of the problem is all inclusive, and his integrity will not permit him to accept oversimplifications. But this integrity and inclusiveness have already produced a body of work which may prove to be the most significant of our time.

It is a work which many readers have interpreted as a shrill cry of despair. But its basic assumptions are optimistic: that man is, potentially, at least, a moral free agent; that he can instinctively recognize good and commit himself to it; and that through this commitment he can transform the nature of reality itself. It is true that in the world of Mailer's fiction most men are defeated by their demoralizing social institutions. Nevertheless, especially in the later fiction, salvation—for Rojack and Sergius, and even for Lovett—is always an open possibility. Perhaps, in view of the history of the twentieth century, that is all that we have any right to expect.

Mailer's gifts are impressive: a superb feeling for style, a remarkable objectivity about his own work, a large capacity for the direct experience of life, a mind capable of brilliant insights, and above all, courage and a willingness to engage the most perplexing issues of our time. There is little doubt that his journey of exploration will continue or that it will produce, if not "answers," at least some of the most searching commentary on the contemporary human condition.

five

JAMES BALDWIN
— art or propaganda?

James Baldwin is undoubtedly the best known Negro writer in America today. He is a national personality, the author and the subject of articles in popular magazines, a lecturer and television panelist, even an informal civil rights advisor to the Attorney General. His reputation rests mainly on his most recent and most sensational work—the novel *Another Country* and the play *Blues for Mister Charlie*—but also partly on his earlier fiction and essays. However, he is not only a popular success; he is a serious artist as well.

If the two roles are not mutually exclusive, they are really not compatible either, and they have forced him to become a dual personality: both a fiery prophet of the racial apocalypse and a sensitive explorer of man's inmost nature. In his role as Negro spokesman he has been forced into an activism in which he does not deeply believe.[1] In his role as artist he is concerned

1. That Baldwin himself is aware of this dilemma and concerned about its effects on his art is shown in a recent interview

with a problem more basic, more complex, and perhaps even more urgent than the problem of civil rights, a problem of which civil rights is only a part. Of the two personalities it is the artist who will receive primary attention here; Baldwin's novels [2] are the major documents in the record of his progress as an artist. But the other personality, the one primarily responsible for his present national eminence, must be recognized too.

Baldwin's public position on the civil rights issue is best explained in his essays. Two years after the appearance of his first novel, ten of his essays from the period 1948–1953 were published as *Notes of a Native Son* (1955). Nine of the essays are concerned with the racial problem, and the time was ripe for a wider hearing of Baldwin's views. The Supreme Court's rejection of the concept of "separate but equal" public schools touched off a nationwide debate which created a new demand for spokesmen for the Negro cause. Baldwin has proved to be an eloquent spokesman. A second volume of essays was published as *Nobody Knows My Name* (1961); and a third, *The Fire Next Time* (1963), was issued on the centennial anniversary of the Emancipation Proclamation. The essays are generally more highly regarded than the novels. Irving Howe, in fact, recently went so far as to call Baldwin "one of the two or three greatest essayists this country has ever pro-

---

in Paris with Francois Bondy, editor of *Preuves:* "Pour liberer les Blancs . . . ," *Preuves*, No. 152 (Octobre 1963), 3–17. In the interview Baldwin speaks of the need of a spokesman to oversimplify things as opposed to the need of the novelist to remain faithful to complexity in order to create truth: "Je me sens terriblement menacé par ma notoriété actuelle: il s'agit là de quelque chose d'hostile, vraiment, à une recherche qui par définition doit se pursuivre dans le silence et au cours d'une longue période de temps. . . . Il est difficile, autrement dit, de se concentrer, de continuer à faire porter son attention sur des questions qui, on le sait, sont d'une complexité extrême, et que tout le monde au contraire souhaiterait simplifier, de demeurer fidèle à ce qu'on sait être la vérité, une vérité qui n'est pas toujours apparente, et s'efforcer en même temps d'aboutir à une simplicité nouvelle, qui serait plus vraie aussi," 17.

2. Baldwin has also written some short stories, which have been collected in *Going to Meet the Man* (1966); they echo, but do not amplify, the themes of the novels.

duced." [3] And Baldwin's essays do have both power and insight.

Although the topics of the essays are diverse, taken as a whole they represent a fairly well defined criticism of American life. Baldwin sees racial injustice as the manifestation of a far larger problem, a national schizophrenia. Uncomfortable with reality, Americans are withdrawing into a vast system of illusions. The ultimate fact which these illusions avoid is "the fact of death, which is the only fact we have," he says in *The Fire Next Time*. He sees this as peculiarly American; denial of the final existential reality is the illusion at the heart of "the American vision of the world," which, he says in *Notes of a Native Son*, "allows so little reality . . . for any of the darker forces in human life. . . ." And this central illusion is the basis of a vast web of unreality in which contemporary society is imprisoned, a web which includes such seemingly diverse responses as the phony ecstasy of the Beatniks and the refusal of the State Department to recognize Red China. There is a national compulsion to avoid unpleasant facts.

Because the American Negro is in conflict with the power structure [4] which defines the national values, he is more sensitive than the average white to the falsity of these values. But to most Negroes this sensitivity, as Baldwin points out in *The Fire Next Time*, is merely a source of anguish: "In a society that is entirely hostile, and, by its nature, seems determined to cut you down . . . it begins to be almost impossible to distinguish a real from a fancied injury. One can very quickly cease to attempt this distinction, and, what is worse, one usually ceases to attempt it without realizing that one has done so." Thus the dominant whites are schizophrenic

3. Irving Howe, *A World More Attractive* (New York: Horizon, 1963), p. 120.

4. Dan Jacobson, an English novelist who grew up in South Africa and who writes about racial problems, feels that Baldwin has not really come to grips with the question of power in America. In "James Baldwin as Spokesman," *Commentary*, XXXII (1961), 497-502, Jacobson says that "Instead of analyzing the consequences of Negro powerlessness, or speculating about the kinds of power they may hope to win for themselves, he too frequently contents himself with making moral appeals, or with issuing warnings," 500.

and the victimized Negroes are paranoid, and both groups are fugitives from the truth which alone can make them free.

Baldwin's essays argue again and again that man's only hope for the discovery of truth lies in the relentless examination of his own inner nature. This, he says in *Nobody Knows My Name,* can be the basis for a satisfactory adjustment to the world: "The questions which one asks oneself begin, at last, to illuminate the world, and become one's key to the experience of others. One can rarely face in others what one cannot face in oneself. On this confrontation depends the measure of our experience and compassion." The problem of identity, according to Baldwin, is more serious in the United States than in Europe because of the fluidity of American society; when men are not brought up with a sense of their proper place in the world, they must fight to achieve it.

In many of the essays Baldwin argues for the feasibility of social action. "If you know whence you came," he says in *The Fire Next Time,* "there is really no limit to where you can go." But as we have seen, he believes that the overwhelming majority of Americans base their ideals and their actions upon illusions. How, then, can they find the truth upon which effective social action depends?

Baldwin sometimes suggests that these illusions can be destroyed if our pursuit of the truth is courageous and tenacious enough. For example, in *Nobody Knows My Name* he says that "a country is only as strong as the people who make it up and the country turns into what the people want it to become. Now this country is going to be transformed. It will not be transformed by an act of God, but by all of us, by you and me. I don't believe any longer that we can afford to say that it is entirely out of our hands. We made the world we're living in and we have to make it over." In one sense this passage is optimistic; it assumes the possibility of constructive action. But there is also a note of desperation in the statements that we cannot afford to believe anything else and that we have to remake the world.

This same note of desperation is implied in the title of his most recent book of essays: "Everything now, we must assume, is in our hands; we have no right to assume otherwise. . . . If we do not now dare everything, the fullfillment of that prophecy, re-created from the Bible in song by a slave, is upon us: God gave Noah the rainbow sign, No more water, the fire next time." Here Baldwin is talking about the urgency of remaking our American society before the racial problem explodes, but his feeling is the same about the thermonuclear Armageddon which seems to lie ahead:

in the end, it is the threat of universal extinction hanging over all the world today that changes, totally and forever, the nature of reality and brings into devastating question the true meaning of man's history. We human beings now have the power to exterminate ourselves; this seems to be the entire sum of our achievement. We have taken this journey and arrived at this place in God's name. This, then, is the best that God (the white God) can do. If that is so, then it is time to replace him—replace him with what? And this void, this despair, this torment is felt everywhere in the West, from the streets of Stockholm to the churches of New Orleans and the sidewalks of Harlem.

A major theme of *The Fire Next Time* is the death of the traditional God of Western civilization. Throughout the essay the church is shown to be a place of refuge for emotional cripples, a "mask for self-hatred and despair," in which the teachings of Jesus have become subverted by those of the "mercilessly fanatical and self-righteous St. Paul." Baldwin's own concept of God is perhaps best defined in *Nobody Knows My Name:*

I suggest that the role of the Negro in American life has something to do with our concept of what God is, and from my point of view, this concept is not big enough. . . . To be with God is really to be involved with some enormous, overwhelming desire, and joy, and power which you cannot control, which controls you. I conceive of my own life as a journey toward something I do not understand, which in the going toward, makes me better. I conceive of God, in fact, as a means of liberation and not a means to control others.

In this passage we can sense the undercurrent of Baldwin's deep desire for submission, a desire basically incompatible with his role as public spokesman for civil rights. As a public spokesman he urges rebellion, while as an artist his inner need is for acceptance. The one role demands social action while the other denies the relevance of that action. Baldwin himself is not unaware of this dilemma. He says, in *Notes of a Native Son:*

> It began to seem that one would have to hold in the mind forever two ideas which seemed to be in opposition. The first was acceptance, the acceptance, totally without rancor, of life as it is, and men as they are: in the light of this idea, it goes without saying that injustice is a commonplace. But this did not mean that one could be complacent, for the second idea was of equal power: that one must never, in one's own life, accept these injustices as commonplace but must fight them with all one's strength. The fight begins, however, in the heart and it now had been laid to my charge to keep my own heart free of hatred and despair.

While the idea of rebellion against injustice is dominant in the essays on the racial crisis, the idea of acceptance of the ulti-mate existential fact is there too. For the illustration, rather than the exposition, of these apparently conflicting views of the human condition, Baldwin's fiction is the most illuminating source.

Baldwin's first novel, *Go Tell It on the Mountain* (1953), is a powerful account of the bleak physical environment and the lacerating emotional tensions of Negroes in the Harlem ghetto. It is focused upon the religious experience of a four-teen-year-old boy, John Grimes, whose life resembles Bald-win's in many details, as readers of *The Fire Next Time* will recognize. But the name John Grimes suggests that his story is intended to have a much broader social relevance.

The novel is very carefully constructed; it even has a Table of Contents. Epigraphs are used extensively to heighten the meaning of the sections. Part One, "The Seventh Day," is an account of the day in March, 1935, which is John's four-teenth birthday. The day culminates in the Saturday night service (which extends into the seventh day) at the Temple of the Fire Baptized, a storefront church. Part Two, "The Prayers of the Saints," enters the minds and memories of the three adult members of the Grimes family who attend the service: Florence, John's aunt; Gabriel, his stepfather; and Elizabeth, John's mother. Part Three, "The Threshing Floor," is the story of the religious experience which overwhelms John with its intensity.

The novel quickly documents the shabbiness and despair of life in the ghetto. More appalling than the physical details, however, are the psychological and spiritual dimensions of the prison. Gabriel is a bitter and sadistic religious zealot. His favorite text, "Set thine house in order," is ironic; he refuses to see or understand the frustrations and feelings of his family. His son Roy, though younger than John, is already driven by hatred, and on this Saturday is knifed in a gang fight in a white neighborhood. When Gabriel's wife tries to tell him what is happening to Roy, he slaps her, and he beats Roy viciously when Roy tries to protect her. Gabriel feels that his position as deacon of the Temple invests him with infallibility and absolute power, and he regards the nonelect not with Christian love, but with thinly veiled contempt. He has told John that his face bears the mark of the devil, and John is vulnerable enough to believe him.

But the book reveals evidences of love too, especially in the relationship between John and his mother. Her favorite Biblical text, amazingly optimistic in view of what Part Two reveals about her past, is in direct contrast to Gabriel's: "Everything works together for them that love the Lord." For John, his mother represents "patience . . . endurance . . . long suffering." She reminds us, in fact, of Faulkner's Dilsey. Her love is all that keeps the family together.

The isolation of the people of the ghetto, simply a given fact in Part One, is made more explicit in the stories of Part Two. Florence and Elizabeth had worked as cleaning women in Wall Street, and Gabriel had worked in a menial position for a white family in the Deep South; but the two races are almost unaware of each other's existence in any real, human sense. This is made most evident in Elizabeth's story. Her lover Richard, a sensitive and proud young Negro, had been picked up for a crime he did not commit, and had been savagely beaten by the police. Identified by a white man who later said that all Negroes look alike, Richard had despaired of living in a world where color is a standard of value, and had committed suicide, not knowing that Elizabeth was pregnant with the child who would be John.

The names Elizabeth and Gabriel suggest that this John is to be identified with John the Baptist. As Isaiah had prophesied, John had appeared in the wilderness to proclaim the coming of Christ and to preach "a baptism of repentance for the forgiveness of sins" (Mark 1:4). The Negro spiritual "Go Tell It on the Mountain" reinforces this identification. The epigraph to Part One suggests a further association with the John in Revelation, who had seen the Holy City in an apocalyptic vision, and who comforted the early Christians who were suffering persecution.

Much of the power of *Go Tell It on the Mountain* comes from the integrity of Baldwin's attitude toward his material. Although the book is a savage indictment of the white world, which has radically limited the lives and hopes of Negroes, the implications of the novel go far beyond that. It is also a searching examination of the meaning of the Negroes' own attitudes. In *The Fire Next Time* Baldwin says that "the principles governing the rites and customs of the churches in which I grew up . . . were Blindness, Loneliness, and Terror. . . ." The imprisoned Negroes sublimate their anger and their sense of injustice in the hysterical rites of the Temple of the Fire Baptized. And ironically, they are seeking a God they do not really believe in, an illusion which becomes finally, in *Another Country* and in *Blues for Mister Charlie,* an even more horrifying reality—a white God.

The consequences of illusory belief are shown most fully in Gabriel. Like his namesake who visited Elizabeth and Mary in the Bible, he is a messenger. But inside Baldwin's Gabriel the message of hope is translated into despair. Unable to see the truth in himself, he cannot see it in others, and this failure has crippled him. His darkest secret is his failure to acknowledge Royal, his illegitimate son, whose death was at least an indirect result of that failure. Although he had felt the "holy fire" leave him, he has continued to preach, and his whole life is now a lie. His fanatical belief is an elaborate rationalization, an evasion of his responsibilities as a human being.

In John we see the process beginning all over again. The force which causes him to fall to the threshing floor of judgment is not God, but an obscure sense of sexual guilt.[5] And there are other causes, less immediate, but equally powerful. Unable to please his father, who hates him as the living evidence of Elizabeth's sin, John is unconsciously trying, through his religious experience, to win the approval he needs and to exorcise the hatred and resentment he feels. He also has a need for revelation—about himself and about his race—and a need for purpose. The reconciliation with the stepfather never comes about; Gabriel's hatred is implacable. And though John assumes an identity through his religious experience, it is to some extent a false identity; no longer John Grimes, he is now just another "saint."

Walking home from the church, John feels that "the avenue, like any landscape that has endured a storm, lay changed under Heaven, exhausted and clean, and new." The experience has had a cleansing effect, similar to the one which Baldwin's later protagonists feel in the physical experience of love. But as John reaches home, "he felt the March wind rise, striking through his damp clothes, against his salty body. He turned to face his father—he found himself smiling, but his father did not smile." The wind, symbolic throughout Baldwin's work of fatal inevitability, suggests what the father's response makes more explicit: that John's experience, dramatic and inevitable as it has been, has not really changed anything. In the Temple he symbolically joins his people,

5. Marcus Klein, *After Alienation: American Novels in Mid-Century* (Cleveland: World, 1964), points out that the object of John's sexuality is his mother and that this is the reason that John turns first to masturbation and then to homosexuality, which is hinted at in the relationship with Elisha but specified in a short story called "The Outing" in which John Grimes appears. John's relationship in "The Outing," however, is with David Jackson rather than with Brother Elisha, who also appears in the story.

but his mission of revelation will involve the later rejection of their religion of despair.

Go Tell It on the Mountain is a remarkable first novel, and a considerable achievement by any standards. The most successful parts of the book are those dealing with John himself, where the prose, like Joyce's in *A Portrait of the Artist,* is a subtle reflection of the protagonist's awareness. Baldwin very skillfully re-creates his adolescent consciousness, and shows the events through that consciousness rather than from the perspective of maturity. The view of the Temple of the Fire Baptized and its saints, for example, is not the view of *The Fire Next Time,* in which the escapism of that religion is denounced. Instead, Baldwin provides the raw materials from which the later denunciation grew, but along with it, he reveals the awe and innocence and idealism which motivate the boy's acceptance of the illusions of the Temple. And through the creation of this very subtle double vision Baldwin achieves powerful dramatic irony.

Part Two, which constitutes slightly over half of the book, lacks the subtlety of John's story, but serves to give it broader and deeper significance. The stories of Florence, Gabriel, and Elizabeth help to explain the racial heritage which John must both accept and reject; they make the experience on the threshing floor inevitable. In the emphasis upon Richard, however, the novel slips out of focus, as several critics have noted. Because Richard is not given enough motivation or credibility, his story becomes something of a tract, and its length disturbs the balance of emphasis in the novel. Part Two as a whole is far too long in relation to the others, so much so that John's story, with its subtlety, economy, and powerful sense of felt experience, is in danger of being lost in this panorama of Negro history.

But Part Three, with its magnificent prose and powerful evocation of the mysteries of religious experience, brings Baldwin through. In the calm of the final paragraphs he has brought the reader through, also, like John Grimes, to a feeling for which *catharsis* seems to be the only right word. Part Three, by returning the story to the deeply felt experience of

John, makes it clear that the importance of the story transcends the argument of Part Two. *Go Tell It on the Mountain* becomes once again something more than a tract: a record and a revelation of universal human experience.

In his second novel Baldwin tries too hard for this universality, and he achieves something less. *Giovanni's Room* (1956) is restrained, objective, almost detached; and what it gains as a formal argument it loses as a novel. Baldwin frames the argument in the reflections of David, a young American in France, who is keeping a vigil on the eve of the execution of Giovanni, an Italian waiter in Paris with whom David has had a love affair. In his nightlong vigil David is trying to determine the extent of his own responsibility for Giovanni's death. The search is a difficult and painful one:

And yet—when one begins to search for the crucial, the definitive moment, the moment which changed all others, one finds oneself pressing, in great pain, through a maze of false signals and abruptly locking doors. My flight may, indeed, have begun that summer—which does not tell me where to find the germ of the dilemma which resolved itself, that summer, into flight. Of course, it is somewhere before me, locked in that reflection I am watching in the window as the night comes down outside. It is trapped in the room with me, always has been, and always will be, and is yet more foreign to me than those foreign hills outside.

During his vigil David arrives at some tentative answers—too late, of course, to save Giovanni. These answers are similar of those of *Go Tell It on the Mountain,* but they are more fully realized and more explicitly stated.

David's trip to France had been a flight from his father, whom he could not respect, and from a homosexual experience which he felt would have no importance if only he would not think about it. In the course of his vigil David realizes that his flight has been cowardly. He recalls a chance encounter with a sailor on the streets of Paris. David had left his face unguarded and then suddenly realized that the sailor had seen and felt contempt for his homosexuality. Yet David was determined never to see it himself: "I would never dare to see it. It would be like looking at the naked sun." His love affair in Paris with his American fiancee, Hella, has also been a means of escape from his real self.

When David met Giovanni in the cafe where he was working and a strong attraction developed between them, he had been powerless to resist: "I told myself all sorts of lies, standing there at the bar, but I could not move. And this was partly because I knew that it did not really matter anymore; it did not matter if I never spoke to Giovanni again; for they had become visible, . . . they stormed all over me, my awakening, my insistent possibilities."

After David and Giovanni began living together in Giovanni's room, David had been unwilling to accept the vulnerability involved if he were to permit himself to fully return Giovanni's intense and unselfish love. Instead, he had regarded the affair as a pleasant interlude before the return of Hella from Spain; and when he learned that she was returning, he had felt a certain relief: "It seemed that the necessity for decision had been taken from my hands. I told myself that we both had always known, Giovanni and myself, that our idyll could not last forever. . . . He knew that she would be returning to Paris one day. Now she would be coming back and my affair with Giovanni would be finished. It would be something that had happened to me once—it would be something that had happened to many men once."

The irony is that this is not just something that happened to David once; it is the greatest love he has ever known. He had resumed the affair with Hella, and as he left Giovanni's room forever, he recognized for the first time the full significance of their relationship: "it had not occurred to me until that instant that, in fleeing from his body, I confirmed and perpetuated his body's power over me. Now, as though I had been branded, his body was burned into my mind, into my dreams." But his commitment to Hella had been made, and he did not realize, until too late, that that commitment had been to an illusion.

This, then, is the penalty of the unexamined life: the inability to distinguish truth from illusion, and the consequent inability to love and to grow. When he left Giovanni, David was trying to protect himself. But this too proves to be an illusion: the affair with Hella is too pallid in contrast to the real love of Giovanni, and the burden of guilt is too great. David's flight only aggravates his weakness, and leads to a more painful accounting later on, when it is too late to save Giovanni and when Hella has been needlessly hurt. Giovanni himself, because his love for David is complete and un-questioning, is completely vulnerable. Yet this is a risk he takes willingly, and gladly; it is the price he has to pay for truth.

Nevertheless, Giovanni's destruction cannot be blamed en-tirely upon David. Like John Grimes, Giovanni is largely passive; his love for David is an unconditional surrender. Giovanni lacks the courage to face the most bitter reality, and after David leaves him he descends into promiscuity in the homosexual underworld of Paris. It is despair at what he has become which leads to the murder of Guillaume, the jaded proprietor of the bar where he had worked, and to the guillotine. Giovanni, too, is in flight—first, as we learn in his talks with David, from the death of his child in Italy, and then from the destruction of his relationship with David. Flight, as David discovers during his vigil, is always a flight to disaster.

Thus both David and Giovanni become the passive vic-tims of fate, symbolized, as in *Go Tell It on the Mountain,* by the wind. Recalling his final flight from Giovanni's room, David thinks of Giovanni waiting for the "miracle" which could bring David into his arms again. But "My feet refused to carry me over to him again. The wind of my life was blowing me away." And in the final scene of the book David reads a letter telling of Giovanni's impending execution, and tears it "slowly into pieces, watching them dance in the wind, watching the wind carry them away. Yet as I turn and begin walking to-ward the waiting people, the wind blows some of them back on me." David cannot escape his share of responsibility for Giovanni's death any more than he can escape the fact of his own homosexuality.

Although *Giovanni's Room* has often been read as a special

plea for homosexuality, its argument is more comprehensive than that. It is concerned with the recognition and acceptance of one's inmost nature and with the sharing of this nature through love. The novel illustrates the emptiness of the unexamined life and the terrible consequences of the failure to distinguish truth from illusion.

The revelation of this message to David seems to be the main function of Jacques, an older man whom David despises because he is now reduced to "kneel down forever before an army of boys for just five dirty minutes in the dark." No longer hopeful of seducing David, Jacques buys him drinks just to have someone to talk to. And he responds to David's contempt by telling him that with Giovanni "you can make your time together anything but dirty; you can give each other something which will make both of you better—forever—if you will *not* be ashamed, if you will only *not* play it safe. . . . You play it safe long enough . . . and you'll end up trapped in your own dirty body, forever and forever and forever—like me." But David does not realize the truth of Jacques' advice until it is too late. David's failure to recognize and accept his own nature and the nature of Giovanni's love for him has crippled his ability to love. It is not just a failure in homosexual love, but a failure in his relationship with women, too, and with the world as a whole.

In general, critics have regarded the second novel as less effective than the first. It lacks the rich sense of life of *Go Tell It on the Mountain,* and its characters are more abstract than the Harlem Negroes. Except for David himself, they tend to be mouthpieces for various views of love and life. And David's background, stressed as an important factor in the formation of his personality and motives, is rather vague and unreal.

Nevertheless, *Giovanni's Room* is an interesting novel. Its atmosphere—claustral, brooding—is just right. The relationship between David and Giovanni, though not idealized, illustrates the qualities of openness, selflessness, and tenderness which Baldwin sees at the heart of every meaningful human relationship. And the denial of these qualities is shown vividly in the vicious homosexuality of the gay bars in Paris.

The most impressive quality of the novel, however, is the seriousness and integrity of Baldwin's attitude: although the book, except in the central relationship between David and Giovanni, is an argument, it is an argument which is honest, courageous, and convincing.

Baldwin's third novel is his longest, most complex, and most sensational. *Another Country* (1962) is tremendous in its thematic scope. The story involves five major characters: Rufus Scott, a Negro musician; his sister, Ida, a waitress who aspires to be a singer; Vivaldo Moore, an unpublished novelist, close friend of Rufus and lover of Ida after Rufus' suicide; Cass Silenski, wife of a novelist whose cheap success disgusts her; and Eric Jones, an actor living in France as a homosexual, who had also had an affair with Rufus, and who becomes Cass's lover. There are several other characters of some importance: Leona, a waitress from a Southern "white trash" environment, who becomes Rufus' lover and whom he drives insane; Richard, Cass's husband, a victim of his own success; Yves, lover of Eric in France, who arrives in the United States to join him at the end of the book; Steve Ellis, a TV producer with whom Ida is carrying on an affair while living with Vivaldo; and Jane, Vivaldo's former lover. Needless to say, these complex relationships provide the opportunity for Baldwin to comment on a wide variety of problems.

Although Rufus Scott commits suicide at the end of the first chapter of *Another Country*, his shadow is cast over the rest of the book. Rufus is fairly well known as a drummer in jazz combos, but has been on the bum for several weeks when we first meet him. Through a series of flashbacks we learn of the affair with Leona, which had been marked with violence from the beginning: Rufus, high on marijuana at a party, first had her on the balcony of an apartment house: "nothing could have stopped him, not the white God himself nor a lynch mob arriving on wings." Although Leona fell in love with him, Rufus felt a compulsion to debase her, and she was finally committed to Bellevue for psychiatric care. Her brother, who had come to New York to take her home, spat in Rufus' face.

The flashbacks also give us many reasons for Rufus' hatred

of whites: the brutality of the police in Harlem and of the white officers in the Navy, the slums in which the Negroes are imprisoned, and the countless humiliations from land-lords, elevator boys, and all the others who guard the white world against black intrusion. The Negro can look upon only an "uncaring earth, uncaring sky." Nevertheless, most of Rufus' friends are white, and his only real love had been for Eric.

Rufus is too honest, however, not to realize that he is re-sponsible for destroying Leona. His friends, who sense the depth and extent of his suffering and at least some of the reasons for it, still cannot comfort him. In the final scene of Chapter 1, he walks out onto the George Washington Bridge and contemplates the wreckage of his life:

He raised his eyes to heaven. He thought, You bastard, you motherfucking bastard. Ain't I your baby, too? He began to cry. Something in Rufus which could not break shook him like a rag doll and splashed salt water all over his face and filled his throat and his nostrils with anguish. He knew the pain would never stop. He could never go down into the city again. He dropped his head as though someone had struck him and looked down at the water. It was cold and the water would be cold.

He was black and the water was black.

He lifted himself by his hands on the rail, lifted himself as high as he could, and leaned far out. The wind tore at him, at his head and shoulders, while something in him screamed, Why? Why? He thought of Eric. His straining arms threatened to break. *I can't make it this way.* He thought of Ida. He whispered, *I'm sorry, Leona,* and then the wind took him, he felt himself going over, head down, the wind, the stars, the lights, the water, all rolled together, *all right.* He felt a shoe fly off behind him, there was nothing around him, only the wind, *all right, you motherfucking Godalmighty bastard, I'm coming to you.*

Rufus' despair extends far beyond the despair of the "saints" in the Temple of the Fire Baptized. He has brought into the open what they can never consciously admit: God is white. If God too despises and humiliates him, then the Negro is indeed damned. "Ain't I your baby, too?" Rufus asks God. But it is a rhetorical question; life has already taught him the answer. In despair, Rufus gives himself to the wind, in what is almost an act of revenge against God, an attempt to confront God with His crimes against the black race. The stars and the lights of the city belong to the whites, and to Rufus belongs only the black, cold water. The water of life in the apocalyptic vision of John of Revelation has become a dark river of death for Rufus and his race.

Although the story of Rufus is well enough developed to be a novella, it is only an introduction to *Another Country*. The spirit of Rufus broods over the rest of the book, and his death compels the other characters to re-examine their own lives. Cass is deeply moved by Rufus' death and goes with Vivaldo to Harlem for the funeral. There she becomes aware for the first time of the black prison from which Rufus could never escape. She is driven to examine her own marriage, and she realizes that her husband lacks the courage to become a really great novelist, that "the book he had written to make money represented the absolute limit of his talent." And she discovers the necessity for recognition and acceptance of one's inner nature: "Perhaps such secrets, the secrets of everyone, were only expressed when the person laboriously dragged them into the light of the world, and made them a part of the world's experience. Without this effort, the secret place was merely a dungeon in which the person perished . . . ."

The taxi ride and the funeral make Vivaldo reflective too. Thinking of the cheap success that Richard Silenski has achieved and of his own comparative failure, Vivaldo makes the same discovery that Cass had: "The question was not really what he was going to 'get,' but how he was to discover his possibilities and become reconciled to them." He recalls his friendship with Rufus and a visit, many years before, to Rufus' home. Ida, who had been a little girl in pigtails then, he now sees as an attractive young woman. Vivaldo recalls that his relationship with Rufus, though close, had been inhibited: "perhaps they had been afraid that if they looked too closely into one another each would have found . . . the abyss." Vivaldo is determined not to make the same mistake with Ida. She responds to his interest in her, and after going to their first party together they spend the night at his apartment.

Book Two opens with the last major character, Eric Jones, sitting naked in the garden of his rented villa on the French Riviera, waiting for his lover Yves to return from the beach, and reviewing his own life. He had grown up in Alabama, a lonely and different boy, and had entered into a homosexual relationship with a young Negro. Although that was long ago, Eric is still unable to accept fully the fact of his own homosexuality. But he knows that he must: "For the meaning of revelation is that what is revealed is true, and must be borne." He thinks also of his brief affair with Rufus, who "had made him suffer, but Rufus had dared to know him," and of young Yves, whose "brave, tough vulnerability" recalls that of Rufus. The thought of Rufus reminds Eric, as it had reminded Cass and Vivaldo, of the need for recognition and acceptance of the inner self. It is this recognition and acceptance which can dispel the terrors which his homosexuality arouses in him: "Precisely, therefore, to the extent that they were inexpressible, were these terrors mighty; precisely because they lived in the dark were their shapes obscene. And because the taste for obscenity is universal and the appetite for reality rare and hard to cultivate, he had nearly perished in the basement of his private life."

Eight days later, Eric is in New York. He has returned from his idyll with Yves to accept a major supporting role in a Broadway play. Although he is reluctant to leave Yves and afraid of the theatrical role, he feels that "In order not to lose all that he had gained, he had to move forward and risk it all." Much of the risk, of course, is sexual; and Eric's next affair is, surprisingly, with Cass Silenski. Both are lonely and disillusioned, she with her husband and he with the isolation of life in New York; the affair deepens and enriches them both.

In the meantime, Ida and Vivaldo have been drifting apart even as their sexual relationship has been growing more intense. Vast areas of forbidden ground develop between them, and Ida has an affair with Steve Ellis, an affluent television producer. Eric reminds Vivaldo of the need for recognition of the innermost truth: "I think you've got to be truthful about the life you *have*. Otherwise, there's no possibility of achieving the life you *want*." And he tells him of the need for acceptance: ". . . there's nothing here to decide. There's everything to accept."

Book Three opens with Vivaldo awakening in the embrace of Eric. But even though Vivaldo enjoyed their lovemaking, he decides that if he were to stay with Eric he would become only a parasite. Cass then calls Eric to tell him that Richard knows of their affair. They meet for the last time in a museum. Eric tells her that he wishes he could rescue her, but that only love can do that. He had used her to avoid a confrontation with himself. She replies, "I'm beginning to think . . . that growing just means learning more and more about anguish. . . . You begin to see that you, yourself, innocent, upright you, have contributed to and do contribute to the misery of the world. Which will never end because we're what we are." She recognizes her responsibility for helping to make Richard what he is. Is there no hope, then? Eric asks. No, she says, we are too empty. We are doomed. As he puts her in a cab, "An errant wind, a cold wind, ruffled the water in the gutter at Eric's feet."

It is now Ida's turn to confess to Vivaldo. She tells him she loves him; he takes her hand, "cold, damp, and lifeless," and symbolically, a "kind wind of terror shook him for an instant." After she relates her own story from the time of Rufus' death, Vivaldo thinks that "at last he had got what he wanted, the truth out of Ida, or the true Ida; and he did not know how he was going to live with it." Her truth is that sin was black and she was black, and the white world drove her to accept its definitions of sin and sex, and indeed to use sex as a weapon. Like Rufus, she had been well acquainted with despair. But unlike Rufus, she had the unconditional love of Vivaldo to sustain her. In the brief final chapter of the book, the plane bringing Yves from France lands at Idlewild. Yves is apprehensive, but when he sees Eric he strides "through the barrier, more high-hearted than he had ever been as a child, into that city which the people from heaven had made their home."

This running commentary indicates something of the phantasmagoric nature of *Another Country*. Unfortunately, Baldwin's recent work—*Blues for Mister Charlie* as well as *Another Country*—is especially suitable for summary because so much of the meaning is on the surface. *Another Country* is a long-playing record of frantic embraces and frantic questions—an almost interminable cycle of sex and psychoanalytic philosophizing. The sex remains interesting for quite some time, partly because so much of it is surprising. Baldwin has written a kind of sexual free-for-all in which almost all the possible combinations among and within the characters are explored: Vivaldo, for example, has a white girl, then a black girl, then a white man, then the black girl again (the girl's brother's suicide prevents Vivaldo from hitting for the circuit, as they say in baseball; he can only *wish* that he had had Rufus). The sexual relationships seem improbable, however, mainly because they are not adequately motivated. The psychoanalysis and philosophizing, on the other hand, are not even very interesting. The excerpts quoted earlier are a sampling off the top; frequently the dialogue—and sometimes the commentary as well—is at the level of soap opera. From the lips of the characters, most of whom are supposedly sophisticated, comes a constant stream of chatter about truth, identity, acceptance, responsibility, growth, love, etc. It is not that these things are trivial (they are cliches because they are important), but that they are repeated endlessly. Not only Baldwin, but the characters themselves seem to talk about nothing else.

It would be unfair to imply, however, that Baldwin was unaware of the meaninglessness of many of the sexual encounters or of much of the dialogue in *Another Country*. On the contrary, he intended the novel as a vision of the modern wasteland, as the title and the epigraph suggest:

They strike one, above all, as giving no account of themselves in any terms already consecrated by human use; to this inarticulate state they probably form, collectively, the most unprecedented of monuments; abysmal the mystery of what they think, what they feel, what they want, what they suppose themselves to be saying.

HENRY JAMES

Another Country is indeed a monument to the inarticulate desires of its characters. It conveys the frantic nature of their search for answers, and the inadequacy of the questions which they ask of themselves, of each other, and of life.

As in Baldwin's earlier work, however, opposed to this despair is a muted hope. It is evident, for example, in the aftermath of the sexual encounter between Eric and Vivaldo: "Then they lay together, close, hidden and protected by the sound of the rain. The rain came down outside like a blessing, like a wall between them and the world. Vivaldo seemed to have fallen through a great hole in time, back to his innocence; he felt clean, washed, and empty, waiting to be filled." This scene is reminiscent of the aftermath of John Grimes's religious experience in *Go Tell It on the Mountain,* when he becomes aware of the avenue in Harlem as "exhausted and clean, and new." But Vivaldo's feeling is achieved only with Eric, not with Ida or Jane. The equation of homosexuality with innocence and purity is also evident in the relationships between Eric and Yves, and Eric and Rufus; it is approached in the Vivaldo-Rufus relationship, which is latently homosexual. In the heterosexual relationships in *Another Country,* this feeling is approached only in the affair between Eric and Cass, which they enter into with the understanding that it will be a temporary matter of convenience.

Many critics have read *Another Country,* like *Giovanni's Room,* as a plea for homosexuality. This only partly true. Although many of the homosexual relationships in Baldwin's work have a certain purity and innocence, he has never maintained that these qualities are a viable basis for mature relationships. They are *achieved* qualities, the product of choices made in the full awareness of alternatives and consequences. Knowing or discovering who they are and what they are, Baldwin's men deliberately choose to love each other. It is the love rather than the sex which is important; the sex is simply the declaration and proof of that love, and an acceptance of its vulnerability. In some ways Baldwin's attitude is reminiscent of that of D. H. Lawrence. In the famous "Gladiatorial" chapter of *Women in Love,* for example, Birkin says "We are mentally, spiritually intimate, therefore we should be more or less physically intimate too—it is more whole." After he and Gerald wrestle naked, both agree that they feel "fulfilled." Although there is no explicit homosexual act in the passage, there is still, as Graham Hough has pointed out, "clearly a sexual element in all this which Lawrence was unwilling to acknowledge"; [6] it is most obvious in Lawrence's imagery.

The homosexual relationships in Baldwin's fiction are usually transitory; they lead only to moments of illumination such as the one experienced by Vivaldo and Eric. The heterosexual relationships are more painful, but deeper. The relationship of Cass and Richard, threatened as it is by Richard's lack of artistic integrity and Cass's consequent inability to respect him, still has an emotional depth and permanence—partly, of course, because of the children. But the relationship of Vivaldo and Ida also has this depth, and possibly permanence too. Vivaldo knows that his sexual relationship with Eric cannot continue; he does not want to become a parasite. This, of course, is exactly what happens to Yves in *Another Country* and to Giovanni in the earlier novel. For Vivaldo the moment of illumination—of full knowledge of the sensual nature of the other man—is enough. His love for Ida, however, is one is which the delicate balance which Lawrence has called "polarity" may, at least possibly, be sustained. In the homosexual relationship it can only be achieved momentarily. It is then sustained, in a sense, by sexual abstinence.

The sexual ideology of *Another Country* is neither explicitly stated nor very systematically worked out, and this is a major reason for its interest; it often has the raw power of undi-

6. Graham Hough, *The Dark Sun: A Study of D. H. Lawrence* (New York: Capricorn, 1959), p. 85.

gested experience rather than the almost pedagogic tone of much of Lawrence—*Lady Chatterly's Lover*, for example. Baldwin's handling of other problems—race, for example—is rather shrill and predictable. Like *Giovanni's Room, Another Country* is essentially a thesis novel in which the characters are given roles to play and points to make. And Baldwin's conception of the thesis is too broad to permit much more than a journalistic treatment of it.

The trend toward journalism and propaganda in Baldwin's recent work was confirmed by *Blues for Mister Charlie* (1964). As Baldwin states in his Notes to the play, it is loosely based on the notorious murder of Emmett Till in Mississippi in 1955, for which the murderer was acquitted. Baldwin's anger at this flagrant miscarriage of justice is understandable and justified, but the play itself is another matter. Baldwin's dramatic sense, his ear for speech, and his command of rhetoric make it theatrically gripping, but its ultimate power is vitiated by what can only be called racial prejudice. Whitetown is a community of sinners and Blacktown a community of saints. The saints and sinners are both appropriately flawed—there are elements of good in the whites and of evil in the Negroes —but the essential distinction remains. The legal process is shown to be a mockery of justice, as it was in the Till case. Baldwin has the State trying the victim rather than the murderer, which is essentially what happened. But he also introduces a Counsel for the Bereaved to defend the victim; this device provides an opportunity for rhetoric, but also destroys the opportunity to exploit the irony inherent in the Till case—the fact that the murdered boy really had no defenders except the ones in the Negro community, who had no legal voice, and the few moderate whites, who were afraid and politically powerless. In the play, the victim's mother had been murdered by white men because she would not submit to them sexually, and the victim had become a drug addict because he couldn't stand the white women who were paying him to sleep with them. And the murderer earlier had killed the husband of his Negro mistress.

Because the white characters, even the murderer, have

some sympathetic lines and the Negroes sometimes quarrel among themselves, the play has a superficial objectivity. But the basic moral contrast between the white and Negro communities is too sharply exaggerated for belief. Although the play purports to be a ruthlessly honest view of the racial problem, it succumbs to the very hatred it preaches against. Its shrill "honesty" is really the cheapest sentimentality; it is not drama, but melodrama masked as social criticism.

Blues for Mister Charlie, then, brings us back to the problem of Baldwin's dual identity as artist and spokesman for civil rights. It appears that, for the moment at least, the artist has succumbed to the spokesman; Baldwin apparently has accepted the role of preaching the gospel of repentance in the wilderness. In fulfilling that prophecy of *Go Tell It on the Mountain,* however, he has failed to fulfill another.

Baldwin's two roles involve somewhat different views of the human condition. In his role as spokesman he is committed to the belief that man's fate can be changed through concerted social action, that Mister Charlie could give the Negro stature if he would only give him freedom now. The artist, however, sees a more complex problem. He sees the achievement of significance as a much more personal process in which each man must try to discover his own nature, accept what he finds, and then involve this nature with other people, through love. Each stage of the process requires so much courage that few of Baldwin's characters can ever achieve genuine involvement. Elizabeth has achieved it in the first novel, and several of the characters in *Another Country* achieve it, though their achievement is more precarious than hers. In the fiction, it is this process which offers the possibility of improving the human condition.

To some extent the roles are complementary; both the fiction and the essays denounce the imprisonment of Negroes by the white world and the web of social illusions we have woven to veil the final existential fact. And both roles are based upon a desperate faith. Asked in an interview for his opinion of the nation's future, Baldwin echoed Camus' view of suicide as the only real philosophical question. "I can't be a pessimist because I'm alive," Baldwin said. "To be a pessimist means that you have agreed that human life is an academic matter, so I'm forced to be an optimist." [7] Baldwin's characters are always talking about the possibilities for making their lives more meaningful, but their few fleeting moments of illumination are menaced by the threatening wind of fatality and despair.

As his first novel proved, Baldwin's talent is large enough to express this tragic awareness. He has courage, an inquiring mind, sensitivity, a very powerful social concern, and a rich sense of style and rhetoric which has strong echoes of the King James Bible. His own personal experience has given him material and a point of view which is worth hearing. But despite the courage and competence of his later work, his first novel is still his best, largely because it is his most honest and most successful transformation of that experience into art.

7. Kenneth B. Clark, "A Conversation with James Baldwin," *Freedomways*, III (1963), 367. In this interesting interview Baldwin also says that his principal in P.S. 24, Mrs. Ayers (a Negro), first "proved to me that I didn't have to be entirely defined by my circumstances . . ." 363.

six

JOHN UPDIKE

– the intrinsic problem
of human existence

The work of John Updike began to appear in the *New Yorker* in 1954. With a degree *summa cum laude* from Harvard, a Knox Fellowship to the Ruskin School of Drawing and Fine Art at Oxford, and a staff position on the *New Yorker* as a contributor to "Talk of the Town," he appeared to have found his *metier*. But for Updike, whose mastery of the fiction of clever sensibility was soon established, the *New Yorker* genre was only an apprenticeship for fiction of far greater significance.

Updike's early short stories, collected in *The Same Door* (1959), illustrate his craftsmanship in the *New Yorker* genre of detached sensibility and mild social satire. His first novel, *The Poorhouse Fair* (1958), is a detached, sometimes lifeless tract against the dehumanizing paternalism of the welfare state. But beginning with his second novel, *Rabbit, Run* (1960), and the

stories in the second half of *Pigeon Feathers* (1962), he began
to deal with contemporary problems in a much more compelling way. As in his earlier work, Updike obviously drew
the settings and characters for his later fiction from his own
experience. The difference lies in the intensity with which
that experience is felt and in the depth of his search for its
ultimate meaning. A chronological consideration of his fiction
will show his deepening concern with the existential problem.

The Poorhouse Fair (1958) is an anti-utopian novel, set in
New Jersey about a decade before George Orwell's *1984*.
But Updike's society of 1974[1] is closer to Aldous Huxley's
Brave New World than to Orwell's totalitarian nightmare.
Through an unexplained miracle of diplomacy, the possibility
of war has been eliminated, and America is free to develop
her inner resources. Social progress has been dramatic, but
largely superficial, and the residents of The Diamond County
Home for the Aged are being killed by the kindness of the
welfare state. The Home is a microcosm of society as a whole;
only after their exile to the poorhouse do these Americans
recognize the void which their formerly busy lives had
shielded them from.

Conner, the manager, or "prefect," of the Home is a liberal
idealist, "a man dedicated to a dynamic vision: that of man
living healthy and unafraid beneath blank skies, 'integrated,'
as the accepted phrase had it, 'with his fulfilled possibilities.'"
Despite Conner's idealism and dedication, he makes one
blundering mistake after another with his elderly "guests."
He is out of touch with their real needs and interests. His
failure is symbolic of the failure of the welfare state itself.
The old people care more about spiritual than social security;
their attention is focused upon the ultimate fact of life which
looms larger now than any other, and which fills them with
anxiety. The former prefect, Mendelssohn, had recognized
that "here they lived with Death at their sides, the third
participant in every conversation, the third guest at every

1. A newspaper being read by an inmate refers to the St. Lawrence
Seaway (opened in 1959) as being "less than a year away from its
crystal anniversary."

meal. . . ." But this fact is the one for which Conner's socialism has no room. In the heat of an argument with Hook, a
ninety-four-year-old retired schoolteacher, Conner contends,
"We've sifted the body in a dozen different directions, looking
for a soul. Instead we've found what? A dog's bones, an ape's
glands, a few quarts of sea water, a rat's nervous system, and
a mind that is actually a set of electrical circuits."

Conner represents the secularization of American life, the
increasing concern with material values. Updike may have
chosen the name to suggest the secular con men who deprive
us of spiritual depth and meaning at the same time that they
enhance our physical comfort. Despite his intelligence, his
organizational ability, and his compassion for his "guests,"
Conner cannot minister to their real needs. He cannot even
understand them; ironically, he is conning himself rather than
his old people.

Throughout the book they compare him to Mendelssohn,
a representative of more traditional values. Although Conner
feels that "Mendelssohn had in part thought of himself as
God," his impressions of Mendelssohn are always distorted:
he knows him only as a poor organizer indifferent to the vital
paperwork of the welfare state, a daytime drinker, somewhat
aloof, insufficiently concerned or informed as to the health of
his charges. The impression of the former prefect in the minds
of the old people themselves, however, is quite different: he
was dignified, deeply religious, and "never too busy to drop a
kind word." Above all, he recognized and shared their fear of
death.

As the epigraph to *The Poorhouse Fair*, Updike chose
words spoken by Jesus on his way to Calvary:

> If they do this when the wood is green,
> what will happen when the wood is dry?
> Luke 23:31
> E. V. Rieu translation

Updike's novel is concerned with the era of which Jesus
spoke: the sap is gone not only from the lives of the people
in the poorhouse, but also from the society which sent them

into this exile. Jesus had prophesied that the women of Jerusalem would eventually say, "Blessed are the barren," and that day is now at hand. Socialist ideals are spiritually barren, though blessed by the state; but truly blessed are those who refuse to perpetuate man's enslavement to them.

The philosophical center of *The Poorhouse Fair* lies in the discussion between Conner and Hook in the sitting room where the inmates are waiting out the rain which has interrupted the fair. The inmates have been discussing life after death, and they ask Conner for his view. Conner, of course, believes that heaven will be built here on earth, by men, and that there is no immortality of the soul, that creation is meaningless except as man invests it with meaning. He ridicules Hook's notions of the inheritance of sin and virtue, and of the efficacy of human suffering. But Hook denies that man is the measure of all things. "There is no goodness without belief," he says.

Updike clearly favors the older view, even though he recognizes its shortcomings. Like Polonius, Hook is a pompous, windy bore; yet his instincts are right, and his philosophy meets the deepest human needs. Hook does not trouble himself with problems such as free will. For man to understand creation, he would have to be God. Hook is content to think that God, in his wisdom which passes human understanding, created man—and that man must try to live in a manner worthy of God's concern for him. The key to goodness, according to Hook, is faith. However irrational and unscientific that faith may be, it offers what Conner's humanism does not: a bridge over the great existential void.

The Poorhouse Fair is a good first novel; it won the Rosenthal Award. Structurally, it is a solid achievement, and it is concerned with one of the most critical problems of contemporary society. But like most of Updike's early stories, it is theoretical, detached. Its characters derive from its thesis, much like the characters of *The Naked and the Dead*—though Updike's characters are far less vivid, and his thesis less challenging.

But in Updike's second novel, *Rabbit, Run* (1960), we

enter a very vivid world. The protagonist, Harry "Rabbit" Angstrom, is Updike's version of Augie March, a young man obsessed by the need for a good enough fate and capable, like Camus' absurd man, of saying no. At the age of twenty-six, Rabbit is a has-been. The apex of his life had come in his senior year in high school, when he had set a league scoring record in basketball. Since then he has drifted from one job to another, and as the novel opens he is working as a demonstrator of kitchen gadgets in dime stores. The structure of the book mirrors Rabbit's life; it involves a series of traps set for him by society. In escaping from one trap he blunders into another; his life seems to be a series of accidents.

His first "run" is an attempt to escape from Janice, whom he had married because she was pregnant and who is now pregnant again. Never very bright, she has now lost her looks as well. Rabbit comes home to find their apartment in a mess and Janice, drunk, watching the Mickey Mouse Club on television. Acting perhaps on a tip from Jimmy, the chief Mouseketeer ("Know Thyself, a wise old Greek once said. Know thyself. Now what does this mean, boys and girls? It means, be what you are"), Rabbit later impulsively decides to drive all night to the Gulf of Mexico. But frantic and confused, he gets no farther from home than a lover's lane in West Virginia, then runs back instinctively to Mt. Judge (Shillington, Pa.) to see his old basketball coach, Marty Tothero.

It is through Tothero that Rabbit meets Ruth Leonard, a tough, heavy girl who has been living in Brewer (Reading) as a prostitute. Softened by Rabbit's personality and sexual skill, she lets him move in with her. But when he learns that Janice has had her baby, he runs to the hospital, unaware that Ruth is now pregnant too.

Rabbit's running becomes increasingly frantic. When Janice, just home from the hospital, rejects his sexual advances, he runs to look for Ruth again. Janice, bewildered by his anger, gets drunk and accidentally drowns their new daughter in the bathtub. Rabbit runs back to her. But at the interment

Rabbit feels compelled to exonerate himself, succeeds only in accusing Janice, and runs compulsively to Ruth again. And after a final ultimatum from Ruth, he runs again, not knowing where or why.

Rabbit, whose last name suggests both anxiety and running, must escape from other traps as well: from the smothering expectations of his parents and his sister, from the demands of Janice's family (whose name, Springer, suggests trapping), from the shallow pietism of the Episcopal minister Jack Eccles and the seductiveness of Eccles' wife Lucy, from the dishonesty and insignificance of his jobs selling kitchen gadgets and used cars. These and other traps, however, are manifestations of a larger and ultimately inescapable one: the prison of an entirely secular way of life, with its promises of salvation through social and economic success. In such a world, Rabbit thinks as Janice watches "Queen for a Day" on her pay-TV set in the hospital, there is no longer any room for tragedy.

Rabbit's problem is largely spiritual. In this secular world, whose values are implicit in the Mickey Mouse Club and "Queen for a Day" and in the stream of garbage which pours from the car radio as Rabbit drives south, he feels like an outcast. His own spiritual anguish is denied by "all the people on the street in dirty everyday clothes, advertising their belief that the world arches over a pit, that death is final, that the wandering thread of his feelings leads nowhere." The pettiness of the everyday world diminishes him too, and he "wonders why the universe doesn't just erase a thing so dirty and small." Sitting in the waiting room in the hospital, Rabbit is overwhelmed by a sense that his "life seems a sequence of grotesque poses assumed to no purpose, a magic dance empty of Belief. *There is no God; Janice can die:* the two thoughts came at once, in one slow wave. He feels underwater, caught in chains of transparent slime, ghosts of the urgent ejaculations he has spat into the mild bodies of women." Confronted by chaos in society and in the cosmos too, Rabbit is plunged into the familiar crisis of personal identity. But the central question for him, and apparently for Updike as well, is not "Who am I?" but "Why am I me?" [2]

That central question comes after Rabbit dreams of "lovely life eclipsed by lovely death," and awakes with the excited conviction that he must "found a new religion." Earlier, standing on a hilltop with Ruth and looking out over his home town, Rabbit had thought that "if there is this floor there is a ceiling, that the true space in which we live is upward space." Throughout the novel, guided only by his instinctive feeling for the reality of this upward dimension, Rabbit tries to find his place in it. And in the other characters, Updike illustrates various possible "solutions" to the problem.

The Springers have adopted a purely secular solution. Although they are members of Eccles' Episcopal church, their lives are controlled by their social consciousness. Mrs. Springer is worried more about what people are saying about Janice than about the girl herself, and she sees Rabbit's motives as entirely practical ones. She tells Eccles that Rabbit "has no reason to come back if we don't give him one," and the Springers do, in fact, give Rabbit a job as a used-car salesman in an effort to keep him with Janice. Their hatred for their son-in-law is carefully masked by social propriety.

When Eccles visits the Angstrom home, we are given a glimpse of the environment which produced Rabbit. Eccles senses the tough, practical nature of the father and the sister: "They'll get through," he thinks. The father, a man of compulsive neatness, says that Harry has "messed things up" and that what he needs is a "good swift kick." The mother loves Rabbit deeply and loathes Janice, who "got him with the only trick she knew and now she's run out of tricks." This habit of

2. In "The Dogwood Tree: A Boyhood," *Assorted Prose* (New York: Knopf, 1965), Updike says, "The mystery that puzzled me as a child was the incarnation of my ego—that omnivorous and somehow preëxistent 'I'—in a speck so specifically situated amid the billions of history. Why was I I? The arbitrariness of it astounded me; in comparison, nothing was too marvellous," 182.

This very interesting account of Updike's boyhood was originally published in Martin Levin (ed.), *Five Boyhoods: Howard Lindsay, Harry Golden, Walt Kelly, William K. Zinsser and John Updike* (New York: Doubleday, 1962), pp. 165–196.

"overstating half-truths in a kind of comic wrath" which Eccles
sees in Mrs. Angstrom tells us something of the origin of
Rabbit's own philosophical obsession, and in the scene as a
whole Updike provides strong evidence for an Oedipal motive
in Rabbit's running.

Eccles, unlike these people, is aware of the spiritual dimensions of Rabbit's problems. Rabbit tells him that he is looking
for "the thing behind everything," for "something that wants
me to find it." But Eccles, like Conner of *The Poorhouse Fair*,
is too enlightened to take the long leap of irrational faith.
He tells Rabbit, "I don't think that thing exists in the way you
think it does." Although he senses the reality of Rabbit's desperate search, he cannot acknowledge the reality of what
Rabbit is looking for; to do so would be to admit the failure
of his own tenuous faith. Eccles' God is theoretical, and he
believes in a theoretical hell of separation from God. But he
must deny Rabbit's assertion that we are all in that hell, even
though he knows that Rabbit is right. Instead, to mask his
own failure and to justify his own uneasy compromises, Eccles
patronizes Rabbit: "Of course, all vagrants think they're on a
quest. At least at first." The implication is that Rabbit may
outgrow his immature need for the real experience of God.
Instead, Eccles emphasizes salvation through good works:
"We must work for forgiveness; we must *earn* the right to see
that thing behind everything."

Kruppenbach, the Lutheran minister, expresses with
authority the argument against Eccles' position which Rabbit
had also voiced, but could not get Eccles to admit. Kruppenbach tells Eccles that if God had wanted to end misery, the
millenium would already be here. The duty of ministers
toward their parishioners is to "*burn* them with the force of
our belief. . . . There is nothing but Christ for us. All the
rest, all this decency and busyness, is nothing. It is Devil's
work." Eccles is furious at Kruppenbach's presumption, yet
deeply afraid that he may be right. Kruppenbach is the
Angstroms' minister; to him Rabbit is a *Schussel* (in colloquial
German, a fidgety, hasty, or careless person) whose behavior
is the least of God's concerns, "one childish husband leaving

one childish wife." Despite Kruppenbach's lack of interest in Rabbit's "case," his view, Updike seems to suggest, is saner than Eccles' ineffectual meddling. Kruppenbach talks of the force of belief, and it is the quality of *force* which Rabbit admires most in people. Kruppenbach and Eccles, then, objectify two religious alternatives: one which Rabbit admires but cannot reach, the other which envelops him in its do-goodism but which he cannot respect.

Ruth offers another equally unsatisfactory alternative. She has experienced, like Rabbit, the death of God in her own life: "It's like when she was fourteen and the whole world trees sun and stars would have swung into place if she could lose twenty pounds just twenty pounds what difference would it make to God Who guided every flower in the fields into shape?" What Ruth has seen of nominal Christians has made her doubt religion itself. One man used to leave her bed to teach his Sunday-school class. She is contemptuous of Eccles' shallow piety (as his wife Lucy tells Rabbit, Eccles is afraid of women). Yet Ruth misses her belief, and she is drawn to Rabbit partly because she sees the same unsatisfied spiritual hunger in him; "in your stupid way you're still fighting," she says. Ruth tries, not altogether successfully, to become a determinist. She answers Rabbit's question about the thing behind everything with a blunt "There's no why to it. Things just are." And Rabbit himself is sometimes drawn toward Ruth's position; draining the water from the tub in which his baby had drowned, he "thinks how easy it was, yet in all his strength God did nothing. Just that little rubber stopper to lift."

Tothero offers Rabbit still another alternative, a world in which God never existed: "Right and wrong aren't dropped from the sky. We. We make them." "Tothero's revelation chilled" Rabbit, Updike says, because "He wants to believe in the sky as the source of all things." The revelation has the flavor of a deathbed confession: Tothero had suffered two strokes since he had taken Rabbit whoring in Brewer; he is now a "smirking gnome, brainlessly stroking the curve of his cane," completely dependent upon the care of his wife, who seems to enjoy her martyrdom. As a coach Tothero had preached the gospel of self-reliance, and his final "revelation" to Rabbit is undercut by Rabbit's awareness of Tothero's paralysis, an awareness which may include a subconscious realization of the paralysis of the doctrine itself as an adequate approach to life.

Together, these alternatives define the boundaries of the modern wasteland, the trap in which man must run, but from which there is no exit. Rabbit cannot commit himself fully to any of the alternatives; he cannot break out of the trap of existence into the certainty of essence. He is, to echo Sartre still further, condemned to life. "That's what you have, Harry: life," old Mrs. Smith had told him. "It's a strange gift and I don't know how we're supposed to use it but I know it's the only gift we get and it's a good one."

In the final scene of the book Ruth tells Rabbit that if he will not get a divorce and marry her, she will have an abortion. But Rabbit is growing hungry: "In fact he has hardly listened; it is too complicated and, compared to the vision of a sandwich, unreal." Going out to buy them some food, Rabbit is suddenly afraid, conscious of the meaning of this latest trap. Trying to recapture his earlier faith, he looks at a church window, but finds it "unlit, a dark circle in a stone facade." But in the next sentence Updike says that "there is light . . . in the streetlights." This implies a movement toward Tothero's "revelation," that the meaning of human life comes not from the sky, but from man himself. Updike then shows us Rabbit's reaction to his latest dilemma:

Funny, how what makes you move is so simple and the field you must move in is so crowded. Goodness lies inside, there is nothing outside, these things he was trying to balance have no weight. He feels his inside as very real suddenly, a pure blank space in the middle of a dense net. . . . the thought that he doesn't know seems to make him infinitely small and easy to capture. Its smallness fills him like a vastness. It's like when they heard you were great and put two men on you and no matter which way you turned you bumped into one of them and the only thing to do was pass. So you passed and the ball belonged to the others and your hands were empty and the men on you looked foolish because in effect there was nobody there.

Rabbit feels himself once more as "infinitely small and easy to capture." But ironically, it is this smallness which enables him to avoid the traps intended for him. By passing off he had made the men guarding him look foolish, and by remaining "pure blank" he has avoided the nets of the various theories which would imprison him by defining, in too limited terms, who and what he is. In his smallness is his vastness. The penalty, however, is that his hands are empty; he is a nobody. This painful paradox is what makes him run.

That Updike had some such paradox in mind as a central theme of the book is shown in the cryptic epigraph:

> The motions of Grace, the hardness of the heart; external circumstances.
>
> Pascal, *Pensée* 507

In his brilliant study of Existentialism, *Irrational Man,* William Barrett makes a convincing case for Pascal as the first real existentialist. Especially relevant to *Rabbit, Run* are Barrett's discussions of Pascal's conclusion, from his analysis of the reasoning and intuitive minds, that man "is a creature of contradictions and ambivalences such as pure logic can never grasp"; of Pascal's concern with contingency; and of his view of man's "middle position in the universe . . . he is an All in relation to Nothingness, a Nothingness in relation to the All." And Barrett quotes these lines as Pascal's "ultimate judgment of the nature of human existence": " 'When I consider the short duration of my life, swallowed up in the eternity before and after, the little space which I fill, and even can see, engulfed in the infinite immensity of space of which I am ignorant, and which knows me not, I am frightened, and am astonished being here rather than there, why now rather than then.' " [3] This, of course, is the concern of the passage

3. William Barrett, *Irrrational Man: A Study in Existential Philosophy* (Garden City, N.Y.: Doubleday Anchor, 1962), p. 118.

in *Rabbit, Run* which leads to the ultimate question, "Why am I me?" And the themes which Barrett discusses become increasingly important in Updike's later work, especially in *The Centaur.*

The character of Rabbit illustrates and amplifies Pascal's paradox. Rabbit's running, though motivated partly by fear and irresponsibility, is also partly a quest; it has something of the spirit of Grace. There is ample evidence of the hardness of his heart (e.g., in his sexual demands upon Janice and Ruth, in his willingness to abandon them and his son Nelson), but there is evidence of softness too. And though his life is often determined by the traps of external circumstances, he often escapes them. Rabbit never manages to attain the state of grace urged upon him by the chief Mouseketeer: "Know Thyself." He does learn that it is not synonymous with "be yourself." Searching for an essence, he can find only an existence—a strange gift, as Mrs. Smith had told him, but a wonderful one, and the only one we have.

This is a cryptic answer to the riddle, and many critics have not been satisfied with it. But it is the answer which Rabbit's story makes both probable and necessary, in the Aristotelian sense: Rabbit's actions are shown to be likely in the context of his character and circumstances, and in retrospect, inevitable. It is in this depth of characterization and in this view of life that *Rabbit, Run* advances farthest beyond Updike's earlier work. Like *The Poorhouse Fair*, it is a philosophical novel. But the power of *Rabbit, Run* is organic: its philosophy is inherent in the characters and incidents, not superimposed upon it. In moving to this novel from Updike's earlier work, we move from detachment to involvement, from observed to felt experience.

From the realistic world of Updike's second novel, we move in *The Centaur* (1963) to one in which realism is mixed with the wildest fantasy. In the first chapter George Caldwell, a high school teacher, is wounded in class by an arrow. He limps to the door, moves down the hall past the classes in French, music, and Social Science, defecates on the shining floor by the trophy case "without breaking stride," clatters on his four hooves down the stairs, across the parking lot to Hummel's Garage, where the owner skillfully removes the arrow, casually sniffing it to see if it is poisoned. Caldwell is metamorphosed from man to centaur to man once again. He limps back to school to find the class subdued by the principal, Zimmerman, and delivers a twenty-minute lecture on the evolution of the earth. The classroom seethes with sex and violence as the principal undresses a girl in the back row, the students kill and eat trilobites and throw BB's at Caldwell, who must pause to whip a young satyr copulating with the girl in front of him. An unusual beginning. Updike, heretofore concerned with the subtlest social nuances, has thrown caution to the winds. And although critics have argued over the validity of its technique, the novel was impressive enough to win the National Book Award.

The Centaur is concerned with three days in the life of Caldwell, from this opening scene to his acceptance of death in the final chapter. The story is presented on another level in the legend of Chiron, the Greek centaur who gave up his immortality to expiate Prometheus' sin of stealing the holy fire from the gods. Each character in the literal story has a mythical counterpart—Caldwell is Chiron, his son Peter is Prometheus, etc.—although the correspondences are not entirely systematic. Alternate chapters are told by an omniscient narrator and by Peter (now a painter, fourteen years later, telling the story to his Negro mistress); there is some reason to believe, however, that Peter is also the omniscient narrator. The shifts, often blurred, from the literal to the mythical, from one narrative point of view to another, and from tense to tense give the book added richness as well as difficulty.

The analogy between the literal and mythical stories is obvious enough, but there are significant differences. Perhaps the most important is the difference in the meaning of the suffering of Chiron and Caldwell. In the myth [4] Chiron,

---

4. Updike's source is Josephine Preston Peabody's *Old Greek Folk Stories Told Anew* (Cambridge: The Riverside Press [Houghton Mifflin], 1897). This volume is complementary to Hawthorne's *Wonder-Book* and *Tanglewood Tales*, which presented twelve of the Greek myths and

wounded by a poisoned arrow, gives up his immortality in order to become free of the constant torment of his wound, which can never be healed. Caldwell, on the other hand, has no immortality to give up, but attains a kind of immortality by sacrificing himself for others.

Peter is the most obvious beneficiary of Caldwell's sacrifice. The identification with Prometheus is appropriate, for Peter, like the Titan, possesses the holy fire which makes possible all the arts. Yet, like Prometheus, he is vulnerable for this very reason. The father senses and pities this vulnerability. Caldwell's fear of death comes not only from his own terror of falling into nothingness, but also from his sense of Peter's helplessness. "He needs me to keep him going," Caldwell says, "the poor kid doesn't have a clue yet. I can't fade out before he has the clue."

But Peter is not the only beneficiary of Caldwell's selflessness. A whole generation of high school students, while taking advantage of his kindness and disorganization, nevertheless has responded inwardly to his deep and real concern for them. For instance, Deifendorf the satyr, an "obscene animal," later becomes a teacher himself because of Caldwell's example.

Caldwell's fear of death was born when his father died. He tells Peter that "when my old man knew he was dying, he opened his eyes on the bed and looked up at Mom and Alma and me and said, 'Do you think I'll be eternally forgotten?' I often think about that. Eternally forgotten. That was a terrible thing for a minister to say. It scared the living daylights out of me." At the same time that Caldwell is preparing to accept the fact that he must die, his son is feeling for the first time the terror inspired by the knowledge that he may lose his father: "for the first time his death seemed, even at its immense stellar remove of impossibility, a grave and dreadful threat."

---

which had been published as four volumes in the Riverside Literature Series. At the end of Miss Peabody's volume is an "Index of Mythology" for all five volumes. *The Centaur* also has a "Mythological Index." Updike quotes Mrs. Peabody's account of Chiron on the page following the title page of *The Centaur*.

Each generation must face this ultimate fact, each in its own way. In his own family Peter sees "Priest, teacher, artist: the classic degeneration." The grandfather died doubting the immortality which he had proclaimed throughout his ministry. The father, familiar with the revelations of modern science, nevertheless manages to cling to the belief "that God made Man as the last best thing in His Creation." In the son, however, art replaces God as the source of all truth.

The scene in Caldwell's classroom is symbolic of the human condition itself: man, aspiring to reason and harmony and peace, is constantly tormented by insanity and chaos and conflict. He is, as Updike's epigraph from Karl Barth says, "the creature on the boundary between heaven and earth." Much is made, throughout the book, of the conflict between heaven and earth. Contrasted with the literal scientific story of evolution which Caldwell presents to his indifferent class in general science, is the lovely mythical story of creation which Chiron teaches to the princely children of Olympus.

"In the beginning," the centaur said, 'black-winged Night was courted by the wind, and laid a silver egg in the womb of Darkness. From this egg hatched Eros, which means—?" "Love," a child's voice answered from the grass. "And Love set the Universe in motion. All things that exist are her children—sun, moon, stars, the earth with its mountains and rivers, its trees, herbs, and living creatures. . . . Men lived without cares or labor, . . . Death, to them, was no more terrible than sleep. Then her sceptre passed to Uranus. . . ."

Uranus, the personification of the heavens and father of the Titans, was dethroned and emasculated by his son Kronos, a Titan, who in turn was dethroned by Zeus. Chiron sees the whiteness of the Earth, covered by snow, as symbolic of the infertility of Gaia (Earth, the consort of Uranus) caused by the emasculation of Uranus; the irrevocable estrangement of Heaven and Earth has left a curse upon all their children: "Sky, emasculate, had flung himself far off raging in pain and left his progeny to parch upon a white waste that stretched its arms from sunrise to sunset."

This hopeless estrangement of heaven and earth, of the ideal and the actual, is the bitter truth from which Caldwell is trying to protect his son. He senses in Peter, as Chiron had in his daughter Ocyrhoe, the suffering inherent in the confrontation of an intelligent and sensitive nature with an irrational and callous world. Yet Caldwell's concern reaches beyond his son; it embraces all of humanity. It includes the entire student body of Olinger High School, and especially those students, like Deifendorf, who mock him most. No one is beneath his concern. A drunk stops Caldwell and Peter on the street late at night and accuses Caldwell of sexual depravity with the boy; Caldwell gives him his last thirty-five cents. On the way to school Caldwell picks up a hitchhiker, drives six miles out of his way, and is rewarded by having the man steal the gloves which Peter had saved for months to buy for Christmas; Caldwell shrugs it off, saying "he needs 'em more than I did."

Caldwell is ridiculed for being naive, for allowing such people to take advantage of him. Yet he really suffers not because he knows too little about life, but because he knows too much. He sees through superficial appearances into the heart of chaos. "Ignorance is bliss," he tells Phillips. "That's the lesson I've gotten out of life." This "revelation," as Caldwell calls it, brings the values of his teaching career and his whole life into question: if the heart of life is truly chaotic and meaningless, then he has indeed been naive and foolish in devoting himself to the service of others. The three days of Caldwell's life described in the book are crucial; he suspects he has cancer, and death appears no longer as a remote abstraction but a real and imminent event. It is time for summing up.

Caldwell's revelation comes in the afternoon; in the evening he seeks out Reverend March at the high school basketball game. He is in anguish over the fate of his soul, but March regards his anxious questions as a "preposterous interruption." Caldwell cannot believe that God could condemn anyone without just cause, and thus cannot agree with the Calvinistic concept of the elect and the nonelect. March replies that the doctrine of predestination is counterbalanced by the doctrine of God's infinite mercy. Caldwell says, "I can't see how it's infinite if it never changes anything at all." March, angry at being distracted from his flirtation with Vera, the promiscuous gym teacher, replies that a basketball game is certainly not the place to discuss theology and that he would be happy to see Caldwell in his study any morning but Wednesday. "Heavy and giddy with his own death," Caldwell leaves March to Vera, and resigns himself to the solitude in which the ultimate questions must always be answered.

In the final chapter of *The Centaur* these questions are answered by Caldwell/Chiron. He is overwhelmed by a vision of the void: "the monstrous tumble of aborted forms and raging giants that composed the sequence of creation: a ferment sucked from the lipless yawn of Chaos, the grisly All-father. . . . His wise mind gaped helplessly ajar under this onrush of horror and he prayed now for only the blessing of ignorance, of forgetting." The snowy landscape suggests the emptiness of life in the absence of transcendent values, Gaia deserted by Uranus. Yet spring exists even in the dead of winter; the small buds are there on the leafless branches. Caldwell remembers his childhood, when, walking with his father through the streets of Passaic, he had heard from a saloon "a poisonous laughter that seemed to distill all the cruelty and blasphemy in the world, and he wondered how such a noise could have a place under the sky of his father's God." His father, feeling the boy's fear and concern, had smiled down at him and said, "All joy belongs to the Lord."

This is the beginning of the final revelation to Caldwell/Chiron, of the nature of immortality: "Only goodness lives. But it does live." It is this revelation which makes it possible for man to accept the fact that he must die. Immortality is not an indefinitely prolonged physical existence; this, as in the case of Chiron, would be endless torment. Immortality is the inheritance, enrichment, and bequest of moral and spiritual values.

Caldwell finds that "in giving his life to others he entered a total freedom." This gift makes Chiron's gift of immortality to Prometheus appear shabby. Chiron gave up his immortality because it had become a burden to him. Caldwell gives his life, which is anything but a burden, to others because he loves them. Chiron's gift had been to Prometheus alone; Caldwell's gift is not to Peter alone, but to everyone he meets, with no thought of the merit of the recipient or the cost to himself. His prototype is not Chiron, but Christ.

In choosing to give rather than to take, to follow his spiritual rather than his animal instincts, to transcend his environment rather than to conform to it, he becomes the architect of his own destiny, and of the destinies of others. In the Epilogue, we read that "Zeus had loved his old friend, and lifted him up, and set him among the stars as the constellation Sagittarius. Here, in the Zodiac, now above, now below the horizon, he assists in the regulation of our destinies, though in this latter time few living mortals cast their eyes respectfully toward Heaven, and fewer still sit as students to the stars."

The final statement that "Chiron accepted death," the obituary of Caldwell in Chapter V, and the enshrining of Chiron among the stars in the Epilogue have led many readers to believe that Caldwell dies at the end of *The Centaur*. There is considerable evidence, however, that he does not. The death of Chiron, of course, is a "fact" of mythological history. And though Caldwell is obviously Chiron and obviously must die (death for him, unlike Chiron, is an inescapable condition of existence), there is no reason why the time of his death must be 1947 rather than, say, 1961 (the date of Peter's telling of the story). The obituary seems to represent the objectification of Peter's fears of his father's death. At the end of the previous chapter Peter watches his father leave the school: "Smaller and smaller he grew . . . at the far door he became a shadow, a moth, impaled on the light he pressed against. The door yielded; he disappeared. With a grip of sweat, terror seized me." This is our introduction to the obituary, which is written in high-school-yearbook prose and which includes many details about Caldwell that would be known only by his immediate family. And significantly, nothing is said about such standard obituary items as the date, place, or manner of death, or the funeral arrangements. In the chapter which follows, Peter, conscious for the first time of his role as Prometheus, imagines himself chained to his rock and receiving a series of visitors. The first visitor/vulture talks to him of "Thanatos. Thanatos the death-demon carries off the dead." Thus the obituary seems to function mainly as a bridge between the first and second halves of the book; as a product of Peter's imagination, it marks the entry of his overwhelming awareness of the meaning of his father's mortality.

In the final chapter Chiron/Caldwell is setting out to encounter the world again. After his recognition that "All joy belongs to the Lord," he thinks of "his wife's joy in the land and Pop Kramer's joy in the newspaper and his son's joy in the future and was glad, grateful, that he was able to sustain these for yet a space more. The X-rays were clear. A white width of days stretched ahead." His recognition that "in giving his life to others he entered a total freedom" leads to a reconciliation of heaven and earth: "in the upright of his body Sky and Gaia mated again. Only goodness lives. But it does live." But with the sight of his old Buick (he thinks of it as the chariot which Zeus/Zimmerman has sent for him), he is conscious once again of his imprisonment between heaven and earth, and "his heart felt squeezed. An ache spread through his abdomen, where the hominoid and equine elements interlocked." This heartache is not the coronary thrombosis which some critics have assumed, but a renewed, painful awareness of his human nature—half animal, half god. And the following lines reveal his awareness that he is condemned to life: "He had been spoiled. In these last days he had been saying goodbye to everything, tidying up the books, readying himself for a change, a journey. There would be none. Atropos had opened her shears, thought twice, smiled, and permitted the thread to continue spinning."

In the final paragraph of Chapter IX: "He cast his eyes upward to the dome of blue and perceived that it was indeed a great step. Yes, in seriousness, a very great step, for which all the walking in his life had not prepared him. Not an easy step nor an easy journey, it would take an eternity to get there, an eternity as the anvil ever fell. . . . His will, a perfect diamond under the pressure of absolute fear, uttered the final word. *Now.* . . . Chiron accepted death." The falling anvil symbolizes the estrangement of heaven and earth (Chiron had felt earlier, "Perhaps—the thought deepened his sickness—an anvil could fall forever from Sky and never strike Earth") in both space and time. It is this estrangement which creates the "absolute fear" in us. Yet a symbolic heaven is attainable, in Updike's view, even though it may take us "an eternity to get there." And paradoxically, the acceptance of death, the acceptance of our human mortality, is our ticket for the journey. In that acceptance the animal part of us dies and we are set among the stars. It is this climactic epiphany, rather than the physical death of Caldwell, which the final pages of *The Centaur* reveal. The acceptance, in absolute fear, of the fact of death is the first requirement for the existential acceptance of life.

Some critics have objected to the mythology in *The Centaur*. While it does make the story more difficult, it gives it added dimension and richness too. It is the perfect metaphor for Updike's view of the human condition: neither god nor beast, man is something of both, a creature on the boundary between heaven and earth, at home in neither. And Chiron's heaven is not the Christian one: it is the home of irrational and capricious gods who have made him their victim and their sport. Yet he aspires to an order beyond the chaos of Olympus, and the gods have entrusted him to teach their princely children. The story of the creation which he tells them, in which "Love set the Universe in motion," is a more poetic conception, perhaps, than Caldwell's lecture on evolution, but it has the same unhappy ending: the Titans are overthrown by the irrational violence of the gods, just as Caldwell's rational explanation of man is drowned in the rising tide of irrationality in his classroom. Both stories are appropriate metaphors for the plight of man.

The ambiguity of the mythical story, then, enhances that of the literal one and helps to save it from sentimentality—always a danger when Updike writes about Shillington, and especially about his father. The use of myth in *The Centaur* is reminiscent of Joyce's *Ulysses*. Although Updike is much more specific, he still does not force the action of his story onto a Procrustean bed of myth. Other parallels with *Ulysses* are obvious too: ironic contrasts between the heroic age and our own (with added ironies, in *The Centaur*, within the heroic age itself), the search of son for father and father for son (and Penelope in both cases is a real *femme*, as Caldwell calls her), the use of epiphanies, and the blurring of time, characters, levels of experience, and literary styles.

Although *The Centaur* represents a narrower range of achievement than *Ulysses*, the fact that the books can be compared is itself a measure of Updike's art. Like *Ulysses*, *The Centaur* is not only a technical tour de force, but also a rich and authentic—even poetic—statement about the human condition.

George Caldwell had found that in giving his life for others, he entered a total freedom. As the epigraph to Updike's next novel indicates, freedom is the theme of *Of the Farm* (1965):

Consequently, when, in all honesty, I've recognized that man is a being in whom existence precedes essence, that he is a free being who, in various circumstances, can want only his freedom, I have at the same time recognized that I can want only the freedom of others.

—Sartre

In several ways *Of the Farm* seems to be a sequel to *The Centaur*. The locale is the same: a small, fallow farm near Olinger (Shillington) and Alton (Reading), Pennsylvania which had been in the mother's family and to which the protagonist had moved from Olinger in early adolescence, where the grandmother and now the grandfather and the father (still called George) have died. Those who have been there before will recognize the landmarks—Schoelkopf's mailbox, Potteiger's store at the crossroads in Galilee (bypassed now by a new, raw four-lane highway)—passed by the Caldwells on the way to school.

The Prometheus of *The Centaur*, however, is now bound. Now called Joey Robinson, he works in New York as a spe-

cialist in "advertising dollar distribution." His mother, now
widowed and dying of angina and emphysema, had wanted
him to be a poet; but his talent and his Harvard education
have led him only to what she calls a "prostitute's job," a
divorce, and an uneasy second marriage. He feels guilty about
the abandonment of his first wife and their three children, he
doubts the wisdom of his second marriage (to an unintellec-
tual, earthy divorcee, Peggy), and he feels uneasy with his
eleven-year-old stepson Richard.

Of the Farm is the account of the first weekend visit by Joey
and his new family to his mother's farm. He is to mow her
hayfield while she and Peggy get acquainted. Except for
the mild heart attack which his mother suffers as she and Joey
are returning from church on Sunday, the visit is outwardly
uneventful. But the weekend is charged with inner tension.
The mother and the wife are natural rivals, as are the husband
and the stepson. And the farm itself is central in this rivalry:
to Mrs. Robinson it is the symbol of her own freedom, of the
freedom she believes she has conferred upon Joey, and of their
heritage; Peggy sees it as a trap for Joey and a menace to
their marriage; Richard sees it as a brave new world full of
fascination. Joey sees it as all these things, and finds himself
unable to reconcile them.

Mrs. Robinson cannot pay her own way on the farm, but she
cannot bear to give it up. Because it has been in her family for
several generations and has its rich legacy of human associa-
tions, to lose it would be to lose her identity. Yet she knows
that Joey, with his new family and his alimony, cannot really
afford to keep it. Although Peggy, still somewhat in awe of her
new mother-in-law, is careful not to meddle, she would like to
see the farm sold in the booming real estate market. Joey
himself is torn between these viewpoints. Although the farm is
a burden to him, there are familiar ghosts about the place.

Yet the farm is not an impossible problem financially, and it
is only a symptom of the larger problem of freedom. Each of
the characters in the main triangle needs to be freed: Joey
from his mother's conception of what he should become, from
his wife's jealousy of his past, and from his own burden of

guilt and doubt; Peggy from her mother-in-law's disapproval and from Joey's jealousy of her past and his idealization of her present role; and Mrs. Robinson from Joey's mistaken assumptions about her devaluation and destruction of his father (whom he idolized) and about Joey's first marriage, and from her own feeling that she and the farm are a burden to Joey. Although these larger problems are not entirely resolved, they are at least brought into the open during the weekend, and all three characters achieve—or perhaps, are given by the others —much of the freedom they need. In their distorted impressions of each other, they had distorted themselves. They become better able to accept each other, and therefore themselves, for what they are.

Since Joey is the narrator of the book, the outward events are filtered and analyzed by his consciousness, and the story is focused upon his attainment of a larger freedom. His wife and his mother, of course, have different views of what Joey is and why:

Peggy's idea . . . was that my mother had undervalued and destroyed my father, had been inadequately a "woman" to him, had brought him to a farm which was in fact her giant lover, and had thus warped the sense of the masculine within me, her son. . . . And my mother, on her side, swept forward with a fabulous counter-system of which I was the center, the only child, the obscurely chosen, the poet, raped, ignorantly, from my ideally immaterial and unresisting wife, and hurled into the shidepoke sin of adultery and the eternal damnation of my children's fatherlessness.

Both views contain an element of truth, but both are profoundly wrong because they are distortions; they "fail to harmonize with the simple, inexpressible way that things had been." Nevertheless, they are the stuff of which truth must be made, for "truth is constantly being formed from the solidification of illusions." By accepting these views for what they are— limited and distorted pieces of a larger, more complex truth— Joey is able to approach a greater understanding of himself. As he begins to free himself from his own misconceptions— e.g., the notion that his mother had "poisoned" his first marriage—he is better able, as Sartre puts it, to "want only the freedom of others."

In beginning to grant this freedom, Joey begins to approach the ideal relationship which D. H. Lawrence has called "polarity." Peggy, the least intellectual of the characters in *Of the Farm*, is the first to realize the need for polarity. In the last year of Joey's first marriage Peggy offered to break off their love affair because she saw that her possessiveness was destroying them. During the weekend visit Joey begins to see their differences as assets rather than liabilities to their marriage. By permitting Peggy to be herself they can achieve a relationship of greater dimensions than if she is imprisoned within his expectations. And by granting her this freedom, he himself becomes a larger person.

The young minister who preaches the Sunday sermon which Joey and his mother attend takes as his text the account of the creation of woman in Genesis. In his peroration he expands upon an idea of Updike's favorite theologian, Karl Barth,[5] that woman "is in her whole existence an appeal to the kindness of Man":

> So Woman, if I have not misunderstood these verses, was put on earth to help Man do his work, which is God's work. She is less than Man, and superior to him. In designating her with his own generic name, Adam commits an act of faith: "This is *now* bone of my bones, and flesh of my flesh." In so declaring, he acknowledges within himself a responsibility to be kind. He ties himself ethically to the earth. Kindness differs from righteousness as the grasses from the stars. Both are infinite. Without conscious confession of God, there can be no righteousness. But kindness needs no belief. It is implicit in the nature of Creation, in the very curves and amplitude of God's fashioning.

Joey compliments the young minister on his excellent sermon, but his mother later calls it "young." She is tired of hearing men theorize about women. And the sermon is rather detached and theoretical, perhaps too far removed from the real experience of love and suffering, from the "simple, inexpressible

5. In *Assorted Prose*, Updike says that "Barth's theology, at one point in my life, seemed alone to be supporting it (my life)," ix.

way that things had been." But in its pedantic way it has given Joey something which he very much needs to know.

In comparison with its predecessor *Of the Farm* is a minor work. Its scope and depth are closer to those of his later short stories than to those of *The Centaur*. Yet it is an authentic work in its own right; and though it is not as rich, as complex, or as compelling as the earlier novel, it is more subtle and perhaps less pretentious. And in a sense it is more believable— not because of the lack of mythological apparatus (which, despite many opinions to the contrary, was an asset to *The Centaur*), but because the characters are more fully and authentically human.

Updike has published three collections of short stories, *The Same Door* (1959), *Pigeon Feathers* (1962), and *The Music School* (1966). Since the stories in each volume are arranged in the order in which they were written, they provide a convenient index to Updike's development.

Some of the stories are interesting because of their obvious relationship to the novels. "Ace in the Hole," for example, is the prototype of *Rabbit, Run*. "Flight" and "Pigeon Feathers" are related to *The Centaur*. From the novels and stories together emerges Updike's autobiography: the boyhood in Shillington, the move in early adolescence to the farm, the years in the high school where his father taught, then after the years at Harvard (largely neglected thus far in his fiction), a year in England, several years in Manhattan, and now the life in Massachusetts. The characters of the novels and stories lose their separate identities and emerge as real people. John Nordholm, William Young, David Kern, Allen Dow, Peter Caldwell, Jack the writer, Joey Robinson—all blur into John Updike. And appearing under various assumed names are the grandfather, the grandmother, the wife, the mother, and above all, the teacher-father who inspires Updike's deepest love.

The stories also illustrate Updike's deepening concern with the existential problem. Of the sixteen stories in the first volume only the fourth story, "Dentistry and Doubt," is explicitly philosophical. But of the nineteen stories in the second volume, three are written explicitly about philosophical themes, and two others have strong philosophical overtones.

Beginning with "Pigeon Feathers," the ninth story in the second volume, there is a decided shift in Updike's treatment of his material; he moves away from the pure vignette toward the story which illustrates an idea. In "Pigeon Feathers" the theme is a boy's first religious doubts and his reassurance in contemplating God's creation. In "The Astronomer" a scientist confesses, somewhat guiltily and almost inadvertently, the fear he had felt at seeing the emptiness of the desert in New Mexico. And "Lifeguard" presents the parable of salvation in terms of swimming: struggle and drown, or succumb and live.

These stories are far different from the well executed but somewhat superficial slices of life which Updike had previously been offering to the *New Yorker* audience. In the later stories the locale is the same, but the concern is deeper.

Yet the approach is still inductive; the concepts arise naturally from the specifics of the situations, and Updike's themes are inherent in the materials of life itself. It is the selection of the proper specific details which makes all the difference: "Details," he says in *Pigeon Feathers,* "Details are the giant's fingers. He seizes the stick and strips the bark and shows, burning beneath, the moist white wood of joy."

Although there is no readily apparent pattern of philosophical development in Updike's stories (aside from the intensifying philosophical concern), there are nevertheless several central ideas. One of these, his sense of the erosions of time, is prominent in the epigraphs to the two volumes and haunts the stories themselves. Time closes the door to the past in which we must seek the meaning of our present condition. Literature is thus a means for recording this meaning before it is irrevocably lost. In the stories themselves this principle is applied in a more personal sense. In "Packed Dirt . . ." the narrator awakes in the night with an overwhelming fear of being forgotten. Similarly, in "The Blessed Man of Boston . . ." the narrator is afraid that his grandmother will be forgotten; this fear is his motive for writing the story. Clyde Behn, the narrator of "The Persistence of Desire," the second story in *Pigeon Feathers*, is moved by this sense of the erosions of time to try to recapture his youth by entering into an affair with his old sweetheart. An electric clock which presents the time in numerals is the most striking thing to him about Dr. Pennypacker's waiting room, and the clock arouses a dormant terror in him: "while he watched, the digits slipped again: another drop into the brimming void." Clyde's clumsy advances toward Janet are an attempt to escape into the past, from which vantage point life would always seem "a distant adventure, a rumor, an always imminent joy."

A second pervasive theme in Updike's stories is the fear of death. The five most philosophical stories in *Pigeon Feathers* are all concerned with death. In "Pigeon Feathers" the boy, David Kern, has been reading H. G. Well's account of Christ in *The Outline of History*. Later that evening, "Without warning, David was visited by an exact vision of death. . . ." This "revelation of extinction" initiates David's first serious doubts about the existence of the soul and the certainty of eternal life. In "The Astronomer" the scientist Bela has seen in the nothingness of the New Mexico desert a vision of his own mortality and a prophecy of his extinction. In "Lifeguard" the divinity student often has felt "death rushing toward me like an express train," and he sees theology as a frightened attempt to bridge the abyss of man's knowledge of his mortality. In "The Blessed Man of Boston . . ." the death of the narrator's grandmother has made him conscious of the perishability of the richest part of human experience, and the story is an attempt to invest her with immortality. And in "Packed Dirt . . ." David Kern, like Peter Caldwell of *The Centaur*, is terror stricken at the realization that his father may die.

Even the earliest stories illustrate Updike's feeling for form and style, and the stories written in the 1960's have revealed a philsophical depth which *The Same Door* did not have. The best stories are the most recent; they are remarkable achievements in form, and their richness of meaning matches that of *The Centaur*. The themes of the recent stories echo those of the novels: the imminence of death and the threat of oblivion, yet the infinity of meaning which radiates from every human experience, and the richness of our human legacy.

Updike's fiction has moved from a rather facile social criticism toward a more fully existential point of view. In a recent but regrettably brief statement on English literature, Updike outlined his own interests in the English novel and then identified what he considered to be its major shortcoming: ". . . no literature is as non-existential as the English. That is, the Englishman does not really seem to be aware of any *intrinsic* problem in human existence. It can all be patched up and muddled through." [6]

Updike's recent heroes muddle through too, but not without awareness of this intrinsic problem. The universe in which they live is an indifferent one where heaven and earth are forever estranged. And man is a stranger too, wandering between them but able to possess neither. He is a victim; his cries cannot reach heaven, and have made earth a noisy hell.

"Only goodness lives. But it does live," Caldwell discovers. And evil is strangely absent from Updike's fiction. Even in *Rabbit, Run,* the darkest of his visions of life, evil is largely accidental. At the nadir of that novel Janice refuses Rabbitt, he leaves in a huff, she gets drunk and, frantic because her mother is coming over, tries to give the baby a bath. The baby drowns. It is no one's fault, and everyone's: Janice's, Rabbitt's, Mrs. Springer's, maybe even God's ("only that little rubber stopper to lift," Rabbitt thinks, and God did nothing.). Responsibility, like the ripples from a stone dropped in the water, radiates outward until it vanishes.

Because it seems to deny the ultimate meaning of moral resonsibility, this view seems unsatisfying, even, at first, uninteresting. There are no figures of real evil in Updike's fiction, only a few misguided Conners and Zimmermans. But it is just possible that Updike is right, that evil is accidental and inherent in the scheme of things, and may even arise from a misguided righteousness. The gas chambers at Dachau and the vaporization of Hiroshima, after all, were the end results of

6. John Updike, "A Comment," *Times Literary Supplement,* June 4, 1964, p. 473.

certain notions of righteousness. Updike shows that man achieves goodness by wanting the freedom of others, and by unselfish love. Morality, insofar as it is imposed from outside, is meaningless.

But the problem of evil is one which Updike will undoubtedly explore further in the future. His recent work has a depth, an integrity, and an ultimate concern which have not yet been generally appreciated. It reveals a mind of impressive intelligence and capacity for growth, and his technical skill has been widely recognized. With two novels which are major achievements, he has already attained a permanent place in American literature; and the only remaining question, which cannot be answered for many years to come, is how big that place will finally be.

seven

Desperate Faith

Traditionally, American fiction, like the English fiction from which it grew, has been concerned mainly with the social aspects of man's fate. As many critics have pointed out, fiction, because of its great scope and flexibility, is ideally suited for the illustration and analysis of complex social relationships. But a more important reason for the social preoccupation of fiction lies in the traditional view of the human condition itself. Most of our earlier literature assumed the existence of order in the universe and in man himself. If society could be organized and administered in harmony with the great chain of being, then man's true function in the natural order could be achieved. Human conflict was seen largely in social terms, because human problems were thought to be the result of violations, by individuals and groups, of this natural order.

In classic American fiction only Melville and Hemingway, and perhaps Stephen Crane and Thomas Wolfe, have seriously questioned the cosmic order, although Norris, Dreiser and others have questioned its beneficence. Hawthorne, Sherwood Anderson, Faulkner, and sometimes Henry James, have been concerned with the problem of psychic order. But all of these novelists were deeply concerned with social conflict as well; and Twain, Howells, Norris, Wharton, Cather, Dreiser, Lewis, Fitzgerald, Dos Passos, Farrell, Steinbeck, Marquand, and countless lesser writers have shown man in conflict primarily with his society rather than with the universe or with himself.

The two greatest immediate predecessors of our comtemporary writers, however, were outside this mainstream. Although Hemingway's greatest influence may have been stylistic, he also illuminated man's cosmic dilemma with the greatest power since Melville. And even though later writers have largely rejected his "code" as a valid response to his encounter with *nada,* the encounter itself remains a major theme of contemporary fiction. Faulkner, whose work is thematically the richest in the history of American fiction, was aware, of course, of man's cosmic and social fates. His work, in fact, has been carefully studied by leaders of the existential movement like Sartre and Camus. But with all its philosophical and social complexity, it concerns above all what Faulkner called "the problems of the human heart in conflict with itself."

Like Hemingway and Faulkner, our best contemporary writers are moving away from the traditional social orientation of American fiction. This is not to deny the value of their work as social commentary; it is the best commentary we have. But most of them feel that man's social problems are symptomatic of more basic cosmic and psychic problems.

Contemporary fiction indicates a far deeper social disenchantment than we find in writers like Lewis, Fitzgerald, Dreiser, and perhaps even Mark Twain, who had more than a passing fancy for the social values which they attacked. The values of "the American way of life," if they ever existed, are now shown to be dead, irrelevant to the real human condition. And their irrelevance is damaging because they are used to spin a vast web of illusion. In *Another Country* Ida says that "white people go around jerking themselves off with all that jazz about the land of the free and the home of the brave." Although Baldwin's Negroes are the obvious victims of this system of illusions, his whites suffer from it too. Throughout contemporary fiction we find characters who must somehow live with public values which contradict the deepest human instincts. And because of the growing power of our social institutions, this problem, which Mailer calls our national schizophrenia, daily grows more acute.

Of all the protagonists of our five novelists, perhaps only John Grimes of Baldwin's first novel moves to an unquestioning acceptance of public values. But his acceptance is undercut with irony because we know that Baldwin regards the values of Harlem storefront evangelism as a system of illusions just as vicious as "all that jazz about the land of the free and the home of the brave." A more common form of acceptance is the resignation to permanent alienation from public values, as in Baldwin's David, Mailer's Hipsters, Updike's Rabbit, and all of Salinger's protagonists. Some characters, like Bellow's Leventhal, Mailer's Eitel, and Updike's Joey Robinson, have made a separate peace, but it is an uneasy truce arrived at in full awareness of its costs and consequences. They have little faith in social action; there are no Tom Joads enlisting in the fight for the proletariat. Bellow's Joseph enlists in a war he cannot believe in, but his commitment, like that of Mailer's Lovett and Baldwin's Vivaldo, is a desperate one—not so much to save humanity as to share its fate.

Political commitment is possible only when society is thought to be perfectible, and perfectibility implies that man is rational and that nature is ordered. Melville had questioned all of these assumptions, but had been increasingly ignored as his questions became more searching. And at the turn of the century Crane, Norris, Dreiser, and others suggested that man was a pawn in a cosmic game whose rules he didn't understand— even though they did assume that there were rules. In the aftermath of World War I, however, Hemingway appeared with a style which could not be ignored, and with assumptions close to Melville's. Hemingway's code furnishes a clean, well lighted place in the midst of *nada,* the same void which Ahab and Ishmael saw in the great white whale.

This encounter with *nada* is a commonplace of contemporary fiction; the universe seen by most of our current writers is a vast, incomprehensible flux. As Henderson says, it is all *strange*. And in it man is estranged—his longing for order and justice frustrated by his constant encounter with chaos and meaninglessness, his finitude lost in infinite complexity.

Of the five writers considered here, Salinger has been the most reluctant to define explicitly his view of the universe. Some of his seers profess to find a rich spiritual order in the apparent universal chaos. Yet Salinger himself is critical of the spiritual exclusiveness of his characters; Franny's "Jesus Prayer," for example, must be modified by Zooey's corollary that the concept of Christ has no real meaning outside of its human context. While Salinger does not deny the reality of the spiritual dimension of human life, he does question whether it should take precedence over our responsibilities to other people. To this question, which is central in his work, there is no apparent answer—and perhaps we should expect none.

Bellow and Updike see the universe in existentialist terms. It has no essence; it simply exists; it is all strange. Bellow's dangling man says that "the stage has been reset and human beings only walk on it," and Leventhal rejects the idea of a heavenly department of weights and measures. Herzog is the first of Bellow's heroes to discover God; but Herzog's search is inward, and his God is not omnipotent but contingent, a flickering inner light. The meaning of Bellow's universe, as Schlossberg never tires of saying, is entirely human. In Updike's first novel the belief in God is shown to be a spiritual necessity stronger than the humanitarian illusions of the welfare state. But in the later work, God becomes increasingly vestigial, a ceremonial idol to be invoked against the void. Although George Caldwell clings to a belief in this vestigial God, his son does not, and both are aware of the permanent estrangement of heaven and earth, with man trapped between them. The meaning of heaven and earth is entirely human, and the feeling that this meaning is transitory gives Updike's work its most moving quality.

Although the emphasis in Baldwin's work is psychological,

his universe is close to that of Bellow and Updike. Meaning-less in itself, it means whatever we believe it does. The white God who drives John Grimes to abject surrender and Rufus Scott to suicide is, like Melville's white whale, a negative, destructive principle only because man has made him so.

For Mailer the meaning of the universe is always condi-tional, contingent upon the vast struggle between the bipolar forces—growth and decay, salvation and damnation, good and evil, God and the Devil—which is waged both within man and in his environment. Mailer's theory departs from the usual existentialist view because it assumes a two-way flow of mean-ing. Although God is created by men, he is greater than men; like Mailer's universe, his God is the sum of human attitudes and commitments. Men, through their existential choices, can increase or diminish this power and meaning. And this power and meaning, in turn, influences men.

In a universe which is meaningless, or at least impenetrable by man's limited powers of reason, man tends to look within himself for ultimate answers. But the answers of our five writers are as varied as their views of the cosmos.

Salinger's characters feel suffocated by a world which de-nies innocence. Although they are critical of themselves as well as society, their concern is moral; they seldom question their own psychic health. In order to survive they withdraw into mysticism, regard the outside world with a love which is largely pity, and try to establish communication with an elite whose code is based upon attunement not to the sensual world of Hemingway, but to the spiritual world of incorruptible in-nocence. These characters, however, discover that innocence is impossible in the real world: Holden cannot save Phoebe from the fall, and Franny cannot hold herself aloof. There is even some evidence that Seymour knew, and Buddy is learn-ing, that to try to be more than human is inevitably to become less—as Bellow's Schlossberg would say.

Updike's characters, like Salinger's, fail to recognize their psychic problems. Even Rabbit Angstrom, the most existential of Updike's heroes, sees his own conflicts mainly in intellec-tual terms; his running, like Augie March's, is the result of a conscious refusal to lead a disappointed life. He is haunted by a sense of chaos in the universe, not in himself. Updike's characters, like his legendary centaur, are caught between heaven and earth. They see a universe endowed with a rich human meaning, and they feel a tragic sense of loss at the erosion of that meaning by time and cosmic indifference. But they assume that a coherent human meaning does exist.

Although Bellow has always been mainly concerned with this cosmic existential dilemma, he also recognizes an inherent psychic problem. Most of his characters are rationalists, but they are aware of, and sometimes dominated by, depths of life which they cannot explain. Joseph's sudden fury against his niece or against some obscure clerk, Allbee's suicide attempt, Henderson's compulsive confrontations with death, Herzog's wild digressions in the classroom—all emerge from these psychic depths. While Bellow's heroes gain from their experiences a larger humanity and a measure of faith in themselves, their victories are always limited ones; and the depths of life remain, with their constant threat of madness. Bellow's characters are constantly confronted with alternatives which involve the choice of psychic as well as cosmic meaning.

Baldwin stresses the given limits within which this existential choice must operate. He shows how heredity and environment place practical limits on human possibilities and create certain psychic realities within us. By recognizing and understanding these realities we can begin to change them somewhat. But the price is more than most of us are willing or able to pay; to achieve psychic integrity we must strip away our illusions and become completely vulnerable. Most of Baldwin's characters have neither the weapons nor the will to fight their way out of this psychic jungle.

Fascinated with the manifestations of evil, violence, and irrationality in public and private life, Norman Mailer has sought their origins in the psychopathic forces of man's deepest nature. Assuming that no human act can be unnatural, he sees murder, sadism, fascism, and other forms of violence not as aberrations but fulfillments of deep psychic needs. The most compelling of these needs, and the one most frustrated in modern life, is the need for freedom. Without it man cannot achieve meaning. But absolute freedom is anarchy; and although Mailer does not advocate anarchy, he feels that it is a lesser evil than absolute order, which denies choice and therefore condemns the soul. To suppress man's irrational needs is to suppress reality, and to do this is insanity. For our national schizophrenia Mailer offers no miracle drugs; he simply hopes that man's commitment to his existential God will have a favorable influence upon his psychic nature.

Our best contemporary fiction, then, is in the tradition of our classic fiction: both see man in tragic terms, beset by doubts and destined to die, yet full of significance and capable of salvation. The major differences are in perspective: man is now shown to be threatened by a chaotic universe in which he is a stranger, by his cancerous social values and insitutions, by his new technology, and even by psychopathic forces deep within himself. In this more sweeping perspective, man's fate assumes a desperate urgency.

The contemporary perspective is relativistic. Man, his society, and his universe have no fixed nature, but are seen instead in terms of possibilities which shift constantly as man makes his existential choices. He must try to enlarge these possibilities in the face of powerful forces which threaten to diminish them. His goal is freedom, his weapon choice, and his battleground the self, where his unique possibilities may either grow or decay.

Despite its well known and often deprecated obsession with the self, modern fiction, on the whole, is not socially irresponsible. It insists instead on a more valid relationship of man with society—based not on the imposition of duties and restrictions by society, but on the free assumption of social responsibilities by the self. Because it keeps real alternatives open, this relationship allows for the expansion of human possibilities and for a more meaningful, positive commitment to humanity. Under a system of social repression man may survive, but only at the cost of his freedom, his possibilities, and his soul. He can serve in the heaven of social stability or reign in the hell of freedom. But only in this seeming hell can he find significance and salvation.

Like much of our classic fiction, the contemporary perspective rejects myopic views of man. Herzog's refusal to accept a "lousy, cringing" view of humanity is a recent statement of a theme which runs through Hester's transformation of her scarlet letter, Ishmael's survival on the symbolic coffin, Huck's refusal to become "sivilized," Dilsey's love for her oppressors. Like Anderson's Winesburg, comtemporary fiction is full of characters whose imprisonment by a limited version of the truth has made them grotesque.

Contemporary writers, finding that traditional philosophies do not explain the experience of our time, have created their own interpretations. Their fiction has moved away from the traditional social orientation of American fiction, and especially from the traditional assumptions about the universe and man himself. But there are many precedents for these new assumptions, and the ultimate assumption is still the traditional one: that man, despite his inevitable and perhaps inexplicable suffering, can find salvation. Like Camus, our contemporary writers are pessimistic as to man, but optimistic as to men. Their fiction is the testament of that desperate faith.

Index

This index is restricted to the listing of substantive comments on the five writers and their work; passing references are not included. Page numbers for the most important discussions are given in bold-face type.